SEAMUS CROWE and his wife, Anne, both retired teachers from Warwickshire, embarked upon a new adventure with the Voluntary Missionary Movement. Their children grown up, they were free, still energetic and hoping to make a contribution.

These letters relate their experiences. Above all, they hope they capture some of the struggle, endurance, humour, good grace and beauty of the people of Uganda.

Anne and Seamus with student, Winnie

The Ugandan Letters of
Seamus Crowe
September 2004–August 2006

The Ugandan Letters of
Seamus Crowe
September 2004–August 2006

Seamus Crowe

ATHENA PRESS
LONDON

The Ugandan Letters of Seamus Crowe
September 2004–August 2006
Copyright © Seamus Crowe 2007

All Rights Reserved

No part of this book may be reproduced in any form
by photocopying or by any electronic or mechanical means,
including information storage or retrieval systems,
without permission in writing from both the copyright
owner and the publisher of this book.

ISBN 10-digit: 1 84748 126 4
ISBN 13-digit: 978 1 84748 126 9

First Published 2007 by
ATHENA PRESS
Queen's House, 2 Holly Road
Twickenham TW1 4EG
United Kingdom

Printed for Athena Press

The Voluntary Missionary Movement (VMM) is a lay organisation whose purpose is 'to challenge, encourage and support Christians to participate in the Church's mission of promoting justice and integral human development.'

I would like to thank the VMM for affording Anne and I the opportunity of working with and sharing our lives with the people of Uganda. I would like to thank especially Edwina Gately, the founder of the VMM, an inspirational leader, poet, missionary; a 'reed of God'.

The book is dedicated to the girls and staff of St Clare's.

Contents

Beginnings		13
06.09.2004	The Snake	18
16.09.2004	Joseph	20
16.09.2004	Sister Sally	22
16.09.2004	The Girls	24
12.10.2004	Leah and Her Tiny Tims	26
13.10.2004	Little Bernadettes	28
17.10.2004	Highs and Lows	30
23.10.2004	Portraits	33
23.10.2004	Blow Winds and Crack Your Cheeks	35
23.10.2004	The Bank	36
29.10.2004	Food, Glorious Food	39
29.10.2004	The Rosary	41
10.11.2004	The Darker Side	43
10.11.2004	Exasperation and Exultation	45
10.11.2004	Travelling Light	46
10.11.2004	The Birth of the Blues	47
28.11.2004	Heads and Tales	49
28.11.2004	Village and Village Idiot	51
28.11.2004	From Arusha with Love	52
16.01.2005	The Returnees	54

16.01.2005	Reflections	56
16.01.2005	Christmas Scenes	58
21.01.2005	Gulu	61
30.01.2005	Give Us a Break: Breaking the Chains of Poverty and Oppression	64
30.01.2005	Bullets and Bikes	67
13.02.2005	As I See It	69
16.02.2005	Winnie the Winner	75
16.02.2005	Incident on the Thursday after Ash Wednesday	77
05.03.2005	Marathons	78
05.03.2005	Death in the Afternoon	82
09.04.2005	Two Scenes from the Bush	85
09.04.2005	Love Story	88
19.04.2005	Light and Dark	90
19.04.2005	This Letter Was Written…	92
04.06.2005	Truth and Appearance	94
07.06.2005	Hi: a Letter Written by Kerunto	98
25.06.2005	Forgotten War (Discarded People)	100
05.07.2005	Country of Contrasts	102
10.07.2005	Latrines, Loos and Laptops	104
10.07.2005	Was It Needless Death After All?	106
04.08.2005	Vignettes of Africa	108
04.08.2005	The Birthday Party	111
15.08.2005	Unruly Mob	113

03.09.2005	Outrage	115
22.09.2005	Touching Rainbows	118
22.09.2005	Forgive Us Our Trespasses	120
04.10.2005	Power to the People	122
04.10.2005	Hell	124
14.10.2005	Dear Emma…	125
14.10.2005	Moments in School Life	128
14.10.2005	The World Revolves around the…	130
20.10.2005	Gulu Walk	132
24.10.2005	Gulu Walk Two	140
17.11.2005	Slip Sliding Away	143
24.11.2005	Cosmic Cosmas	146
29.11.2005	Shall We Dance?	148
08.03.2006	Disasters and Delights	150
10.03.2006	Poor Little B—s	152
16.03.2006	The Tank	154
30.03.2006	None So Blind	157
30.03.2006	I Love Lucy	159
12.06.2006	Enraptured and Enraged	162
21.06.2006	Gulu: Conflicting Emotions	164
26.06.2006	Oops!	170
14.07.2006	In Praise of Youth	172
15.07.2006	End of Project Report	174
26.07.2006	Wheels within Wheels	179
26.07.2006	Books, Bricks, Canvas and Porridge	181

02.08.2006	Dreams	182
02.08.2006	Incidents	184
13.08.2006	And Now the End Is Near…	186
13.08.2006	Uganda	188
23.08.2006	Litany	191

Beginnings

I am now looking out at a grey hen scratching around the trees and the shrubs outside the house. The sun is shining; it is very hot: hot, but bearable, because we have a door at either side of the house, open, with protective mosquito covering, so that there is a flow of air (just). It is Saturday afternoon at 3.10 p.m. and the loudest sound is from the fridge (power is on!) and the cistern in the loo. It is still and silent; no traffic, except the occasional bicycle on the dirt road running parallel to our compound, about twenty yards from the house.

First impressions

It is everything I expected; it is nothing like I expected. It is Ireland or England fifty years ago; the pace is slow, the tempo mute, the time... an ocean.

Never mind 'see Naples and die'; see Kampala and learn the meaning of mortality, fear, terror and death! Drivers trained in the school of Kamikaze. If there are rules of the road, I did not discern them. Little Sister Antoinette (sixty-four) drove on, through and over, oblivious to the mortal peril we were in, and did not even observe my frequent acts of alarmed contrition.

But the sight and sound and smell of Kampala! The convent is an oasis set in the wrong side of town, 'the other side of the tracks': clear, cool, serenely welcoming. The meals are simple; tasty; beautifully cooked; served with grace, literally and metaphorically. The sisters have discovered a potion of eternal youth. Sr Cosmas is seventy-nine going on nineteen; runs around the shops; has a sharp brain, an aura of authority, a huge heart; is tirelessly and endlessly working with nursery children, infants and secondary children and is about to set up an adult group! She works energetically, every day, and all this is leavened with a lively, lovely sense of humour.

Sr Antoinette is shy; quiet; again tireless, working every day with the most marginalised, with prisoners, prisoners with AIDS and with the 'condemned' (sends a shiver down your spine), those waiting to die. Let them talk glibly, those who want the return of the death penalty.

The priest, an African priest of great years and experience, who celebrated Mass this morning in the small and very beautiful chapel, was so full of love, commitment and passion; a mystic.

'You must love intensively; you must love extensively.'

Alongside the road from Entebbe to Kampala, a distance of perhaps twenty miles, the settlements and houses; what can you say? Everywhere is full of red dust; Uganda is made of red dust! Although there are a few good houses, the vast majority are what we would consider to be slums, or worse than slums, made of wattle and daub, or brick, or wood or tin, and in front of them piles of broken bricks, litter and the detritus of an overcrowded city; a sight to make you catch your breath... and yet, and yet... the sight, at 7 a.m., of astonishingly beautiful, beautiful children, infants, tiny dots, primary, junior, secondary, walking to school in such bright, gleamingly clean, gorgeous uniforms, uniforms red, or green, or blue, or orange, or whatever. Brilliant. A mystery.

There follows an account of trying to clear my books sent by freight, where I ran up against the world-wide disease known as bureaucracy! Five hours filling in forms and 'please come back tomorrow'!

So to the kitchen to make a meal: an omelette and what they call 'Irish' potatoes. We'd have something else, but the oven doesn't work; it's called improvisation. I think, at last, the Lord is trying to teach me patience.

'Are all the roads in England tarmaced?' she asked, and her eyes opened wide with astonishment when we said yes. Anne said we wouldn't call this a road but a track, but to Betty, the young head teacher, all tracks in Uganda are roads. There is one main road, between Kampala and Mbale, which is tarmaced, of which she and all of Uganda are justly proud. But for all roads to be tarmaced; well, what a wonder!

Sunday 14 August

What a Mass! What a celebration! Feast of the Assumption.

Open-air Mass with hundreds of people (remember, this is a rural district), some sitting at desks, some spreading cloths on the ground, some standing. Everyone dressed in their finery ('when you go to visit God, you must dress properly'), though some are barefoot. The ladies with their colourful dresses, some with padded shoulders that would put Bette Davis to shame, shoulders so high they were like bats' wings. I learned later that this is a traditional dress.

Then, to our surprise, the wedding party. A few musical high-pitched whoops, like red Indians, followed by the tinkling of a bell, and the bride arrived, all dressed in white, with a white veil and flowers on the side of her veil; the driver with a bunch of flowers in his button hole. She arrived, side-saddle, on the back of a bicycle, but I must stress that there was nothing incongruous in this, nothing comical; it seemed entirely joyous and appropriate. Her dignified father arrived on the back of another bicycle.

The second wedding party arrived in exactly the same fashion, but this party was clearly not as affluent as the first. The bride (poor thing looked miserable throughout) was not as elegantly dressed and looked rather stoic, whereas the first, while not blushing, was flushed with pride.

The most wonderful thing about the service was the exuberance and excitement, with the high-pitched musical whooping; the mothers and the women dancing across in front of the altar, with that electric and captivating rhythm that makes you want to join in. Our weddings may cost a thousand times more money, but they lack that verve, that involvement of the whole community, and the sharing and joy of the villagers. When the bridegrooms recited their vows in their own local language from the official Luganda, it was the cause of much merriment and mirth among the men, but in a very good-natured way.

And then a very moving moment. The service lasted forever, the prayers of a lifetime, but when the official service was over, the couples finally wed, a prayer was said over the celebrants and, just as in an ordination, the whole congregation of men, women and children extended their hands over them in a final prayerful benediction.

At the end of the four-hour service (!), the priest invited Anne and me as guests to address the congregation. Anne was gracious and sweet, and congratulated the happy couples. I asked, since I, along with other married couples, had renewed my marriage vows in a language I did not understand a word of, would that entitle me to another dowry? The priest first looked startled, then alarmed, and said, 'No.' Not quite caught my sense of humour yet.

Returned home, having smiled benignly at goodness knows how many people; I felt like the Queen Mother. It was like yesterday, when we went to the local market: people, children, women, men, would look at us, our faces, some blatantly, some slyly, some with real wonder: so that's what white people look like. Self-conscious, embarrassed, I felt the urge to proclaim that I was by no means the best representative of Western male pulchritude, or indeed representative of any pulchritude! Lads, the responsibility was too much. But, to my shame, I will say this: we aroused curiosity, even humour or delight, but no derision and not one ounce of hostility. Would that were the case in the West.

Our life here is ruled by mozzies. We live on the edge of swamps. Although we have nets over our beds, protective mesh covering our windows, searchlights and machine guns, one still got under Anne's net, flew by her ear, woke her and bit her. I was awoken by the terrible cry of a banshee in pain, or the loudest bat released from hell, and, putting on the light, having done justice to an Olympic high jumper, we both searched but failed to find the bugger. I hasten to add that, if it had been me who was attacked, Anne would have been awakened by an even shriller scream of terror, with some colourful language to boot!

One word of warning: I had thought that mozzies were the fighter pilots of the insect world, zimming through the air, guns loaded, swooping, buzzing down, angry, goggle-eyed and fearless. Not so. Not so. Not at all. Run silent. Run deep. They are sneaky, silent, sly submarines, waiting in the dark to unleash their torpedoes, or like assassins, crawling up behind you to slit your throat. Ugh!

'Jerusalem, Jerusalem. How often I would have gathered you under my wings, as a hen does her chicks, and you would not.'

A scene outside the house: a tropical storm; a hen with her chicks gathered under her for protection. Wow! Bible alive!

PS One tragic, nay, catastrophic tale. All the way to Africa, all the way to the other side of the world, and the young African teacher next door to me is… an Arsenal supporter. An Arsenal supporter!

06.09.2004 The Snake

There we were, sitting in the front room of the house, discussing at length the plan for the school development in the next term and year: lesson observation, appraisals, audits etc., etc.: riveting stuff.

A young girl outside the house shouts something through the open door, which has, of course, the mosquito screen. The head's eyes dart to the door. Crowe's eyes scramble in pursuit just in time to glimpse a flash of a long green thing, a bright bright green thing, disappearing between the beer crate and the fridge (what's a beer crate doing in my house?). When it is said that there was a flash of this green thing disappearing, it does not do justice to the speed; it was like Linford Christie with the runs!

Up jumped the head. Up farther, much farther, jumped Crowe. Anne brought all the coolness, courage and experience of a citizen of a once proud empire: she fled.

This young slip of a girl, the head, runs out to the kitchen and grabs a broom handle. Crowe, at this time, behaves as fully expected. If he had hairs on the top of his head, they would have been standing on end. His scalp was standing, however, fully to attention, and his eyes were transfixed, as indeed his whole body was, in a state of *rigor mortis*.

The head flays at the snake, calling for Capata, the genial, generally always-grinning handyman. He enters the room with a stick in his hand and tilts the fridge IN BARE FEET. The wee lassie dives in: bang, bang, wallop, wallop, wallop, snake dead.

Smiles all round, except Crowe, whose facial mobility is temporarily frozen. Head is hailed as mighty hunter.

Later, Dominic, a young male teacher, looks at the snake and utters the terrifying words, 'Ah, yes, there are many snakes around here, especially from that field (next to the house). Always keep that door closed. That snake is particularly dangerous, particularly poisonous. If you are bitten, be very quick getting to the hospital… otherwise…'

Crowe has built a moat around the house and erected a notice, a polite notice, stating that no casual hawkers or snakes are allowed.

You know, there is a lot to be said for the boredom of Bulkington.

16.09.2004 Joseph

A tall, well-built, handsome, open-faced, bright-eyed, readily-grinning animated personality, full of energy, charisma and go. An Englishman through and through, and a citizen: a compassionate and passionate citizen of the world.

Joseph, or Joe, trained as an engineer. Then, from engineering, he joined the management side of John Lewis as a project manager, where he was highly successful and fully appreciated. And then... and then he did a favour for a friend and came to assess the needs of an abandoned babies' home in Uganda. Five days. A brief five days. No time at all. A blink of an eye. His friend, who worked for a voluntary organization, was double-booked. What the heck is five days? Yeah, sure he'd assess, write a business plan, and *whoosh*.

That was nineteen months ago.

Joe came, saw, conquered. He arrived at the home (first founded in 1929), saw what was, collected the evidence and, although deeply shocked, went home and wrote the business plan.

Well, he couldn't just deliver a business plan; he'd better go back for a month and show them how to implement it... Well, he'd better stay for six months to get it really going... Hey, these were his project and his kids and he was here to make them safe and well. Well?

By this time, Joe, who was completely alone, came to the attention of good old VMM, who saw what he was doing and the immense value of it and stepped in to support him.

It is difficult to describe or do justice to the problems the home faced. The skeleton staff (in both senses of the word) had not been paid for two months. They were running out of milk, and then the water was cut off. The septic tank had not been emptied; there had been a flood, and it had overflowed. There was no staff training in hygiene or baby care, and the kitchen was a health hazard. It is best left to the imagination the sight, sound and smell in which the babies had to live.

The first thing Joe did was empty the septic tank, restore the water and get the place cleaned up. Then, by badgering, begging and chasing funds and sponsorship from all over (a German charity came to the rescue; there are charities from all over Europe aiding Africa), he completed a huge engineering task of linking the home to the main sewer, which involved digging into the mountainside and digging massive trenches of up to fifteen feet all round the very large compound. Wow!

Then the water: restored, permanent. The training of the staff, securing money for their salary, hiring a bursar, getting a laundry going, pursuing more funds.

The babies range from one day old to the age of four and a half. They are abandoned: found in sewers, on rubbish tips, outside toilets, anywhere. There are about fifty at present.

The little ones are kept in cots in a lovely nursery (now being decorated by a volunteer, whose friends in England are supporting her by sending £40 per month) and the beautiful creatures respond with smiles and gurgles when you speak to them.

The workers and volunteers (there are two VMs on site) clean, feed, interact with, teach and love them. And Joe just adores them.

Joe has started up an income generation scheme using local artists and selling batique pictures and cards, and all profits go to the home. He has nearly finished building a new kitchen, dining room and laundry. He is involved with the local community, and, because the children have to leave the home at four or five to go to the state orphanage, he is in the process of setting up a fostering scheme. One little three-year-old handicapped girl is about to be fostered by a local European lady, who came to offer help, was asked to feed the little one, over the weeks bonded with her, and there you go. Another little one is being adopted by a Dutch couple who have lived in Uganda for two years.

We can't tell you how moved, impressed and humbled we were by this wonderful, practical and imaginative enterprise.

16.09.2004 Sister Sally

A huge wave of nausea passed through her body. Every time she put her foot to the ground, a spasm of agonising pain shot through her foot; putting any weight on it, even the small amount carried by her small frame, was excruciating. And on this road in Kampala, rough, dirty, uneven, dusty, it was indeed a nightmare. Sick, light-headed, near delirium, she inched her way towards the hospital.

She should, deep down she knew, have asked to be driven or taken, and there were many who would have gladly obliged. But that would mean putting someone out, drawing attention to her need or even her pain. All fifty-nine years of her life had been spent otherwise; all fifty-nine putting others first, serving others, dedicated to others, for in that way she served her loving Lord.

Born in South Africa, of white parents, in a country torn by apartheid and bitterness, she was brought up in a house of love and warmth and generosity. She took those gifts from her parents, became a nun, and spent a life dedicated to her Africa and her beloved brothers and sisters, bringing them great respect, skill, zeal, comfort and above all practical help; she was nothing if not practical.

The last five years had been spent in Uganda, in Kabala, and she was on a short break in Kampala. That morning of the 20 August, she went to Mass, and Sr Lydia noticed her pain, but, before she could get to her, Sr Sally slipped away. Now she was on the road to the hospital, driven because she could no longer bear the pain; exhausted, drained.

A 'boda-boda' man saw her and insisted he would take her to the hospital. He saw the pain drain the energy and life from her face and weakened body. Like the Samaritan, he was moved to pity. No Ugandan would believe a boda-boda man, in this country of great poverty where each boda-boda man fights for every passenger he can get on his motorbike; where they scour the horizon for every ride and are experts in squeezing every last shilling they can get, especially from *msungus* (white people). Yet he was moved to pity.

When they arrived at the hospital, he refused any money.

The infection was deep. Her foot was gangrenous. They immediately gave her penicillin. She had a bad reaction, had a bad asthma attack and died. Sally was renowned amongst her peers, not only for her gentleness, kindness, her get-up-and-go, and practicality, but for her lack of possessions and her poverty. She had only one skirt and one cardigan. They would pull her leg about it. Now she was free from possessions.

After a life of service, it is so fitting that the last human being she encountered was touched by that grace, charity and kindness she had in such abundance. It is as if her loving master and brother had lifted her up and driven her gently to her rest.

Sister Sally died on the 20 August 2004 in St Francis's hospital, Kampala.

Later on in the week, we met with Sister Sally's companions from her order. One had been a friend since her schooldays. She told us of the extraordinary funeral in Kabala. They had driven for eight hours over a terrible road, talking of Sally's specialness. When they arrived, the road was lined with hundreds of people from all the villages around. There were, they thought, a thousand. They had all come to pay their respects to Sally and mourn her.

What did Sally do? Everything. She taught in the secondary school, had classrooms built, had toilets built, ran a farm for her 'boys' with pigs and rabbits, ran a dance club for disabled children and was starting an adult group. When she saw a need, 'she just did it'.

They stayed all night with the body, sleeping in the village, in the church, in the open air. And the next day. And the next night, and so on for four nights. Even after the funeral, the boys would not disperse because 'We have not yet finished comforting one another.'

In his eulogy, the bishop said, 'You all loved Sister Sally. If you love her, go, live like her.'

Amen!

16.09.2004 The Girls

We had a long, informal chat with the young head, the wise head, the vastly experienced in life head, the head who carries enormous responsibility on her young shoulders with grace and humour. She has been head since January. There may well be one or two things we can contribute, but she seems to be a rock.

As I understand it, the situation is analogous to that of the abandoned babies' home; there is the same pressing need to rescue.

The school is a lifeboat sailing on the sea of Uganda, and it is a dangerous sea. The waters are full of predators: sharks, snakes, poisonous creatures 'seeking whom they may devour'. The girls are subject to incredible hazards all through their young lives. There is enormous peer pressure to have sex when they return home for their holiday, sometimes even pressure from their relatives. If they survive that and make it to university, poverty will often drive them to prostitution to buy their books, accommodation, food. They become the high-class prostitutes.

Men see girls as prey, and not only is bigamy common, but successful men will have several 'concubines' (an old-fashioned word indeed), whilst their uneducated wives remain in the village.

I read in the national paper that, in one district, 77.1% of the girls engage in commercial sex (where is the 0.1% from?). Some girls even in our school have had experience in sex; some have become pregnant and worse: infected.

HIV and AIDS are rampant. The girls are forever being warned that they are six times more vulnerable than boys. The message is direct, sharp and open. On the last day, the head spelled it out yet again: the world is full of danger, with many enemies, waiting like the army ants to attack.

It is like being in a lifeboat, throwing out life jackets. When they are at school, the parents think the girls are safe, in a haven; but one step outside!

As with many of the problems all over the world, we can become overwhelmed; feel the sheer futility of what we are doing, the uselessness, bailing out water with a bucket whilst the ship founders. But we cannot live or act like that: these lovely girls, and the girls all over Uganda, are not bad girls; they are victims. They are lovely, and it is our task to help them to realise how loved and lovely they are.

As one of the Desert Fathers once said: 'You may look down on and condemn any harlot you like, if you dare!'

12.10.2004 Leah and Her Tiny Tims

Leah, Leah, Leah. Lovely, lovely Leah. Slight, young Kenyan, with an angel face and the hint of a lisp (why is it, by definition, lisps are either intensely irritating or absolutely charming? Hers is charming), a Franciscan nun who runs the Leonard Cheshire home just up the road, the rough, uneven road that would not pass for a farmer's dirt track at home, and who is surrounded by her 'angels'. The children are from the outlying district, paraplegics or children with spina bifida etc., all about to have or who have just had operations, all receiving physiotherapy. The home is a rehabilitation home, and many of the children, who range in age from under five to teenagers, are abandoned because the villagers view them as a bad omen and might even try to kill them. But in them Leah sees the face of 'God'.

The home ('The children are so happy') tries to be self-sufficient and otherwise relies on Providence. Leah rears turkeys and pigs and has a cow, and some of the young boys use a knitting machine to make school uniforms for the local schools, a skill taught to them by a kind deaf mute who comes to teach them. I saw two Tiny Tims, eight or nine years old, at work. It would break your heart, but they were happily at work. Dickens in the flesh.

She was very pleased to have received, from a charitable organisation of young English farmers, the gift of beds for the children. How wonderful. The fact that the roof has holes in it and, when there is a storm, the beds have to be manoeuvred accordingly did not seem to bother her unduly. Also, they have five nets, which they distribute to the children after they've got malaria; they can't afford fifty nets: it would be over £50. And there is another problem: the children badly need a water pump, because the last one was stolen. If anything is not tied down with a rock, it is stolen, as the people are so poor. She wanted desperately to have a water pump, but with a big rock to keep it safe.

For a long time, I wrestled with the mental picture of a pump tied down with a big rock, until it finally hit me that her lisp had lent her a Chinese flavour; the big rock was, of course, a big LOCK. Ah. Once more, the light breaks through into the dim recesses of the Crowe mind.

I was poorly last week and had to take to my bed for a day. Sister Leah dropped in and prayed over me. It was like having your own individual saint talking to her personal best friend and asking Him to take special care of you. When she left, I hardly dared to look God in the eye!

Leah does not know it yet, but we're gonna rock 'n' roll. Or should that be lock 'n' loll?

13.10.2004 Little Bernadettes

An ear-piercing scream; a series of screams in the middle of the night. Total, total black; only this screech of an animal in extreme pain and terror. Not a small animal, by the sound. What was it? What had stalked it, or wounded it, or cornered it? Trapped, caught, terrorised. Disturbing, to say the least.

The next morning, a search around the perimeter of the house revealed nothing: no carcass, no bones, no feathers, no skin or bone or blood. No sign of anything untoward.

Later in the day, in the sun-splitting afternoon, the same terrifying and terrified cry. The immediate search to find the source of this cry led to the infirmary. Several girls huddled outside, looking in, and, on entering, the nurse and the deputy head were to be found. The source of the cry, the howl, was, in fact, a girl, a girl called Phyllis. In tones of complete matter-of-factness, I was informed that the girl was possessed by her uncle. Some girls get malaria; some girls get colds or flu; some girls even get pregnant, and some girls get possessed.

The girl's father arrived, took out his rosary, stayed with her, prayed over her, and talked and talked and talked to her. It took much talking to calm her down. It appears that this was not nearly the first time this had happened to the poor child. Her uncle's spirit was angered by the neglect he had endured in his last illness, and was angered by the lack of care shown to his children.

The child spoke in his voice.

When I suggested (strongly) that the girl should be taken to the hospital, I was informed that they would do nothing for her. When I asked if the priest had been informed, I was met with a look of bemusement, if not incredulity.

This happens. This is not out of the ordinary.

In later discussions, it emerged that, indeed, several children suffered these 'setbacks'. The trouble was in discerning which were genuine and which were hysteria or self-induced: the

Witches of Salem *a la* the Crucible mode. I am very sceptical about most of them and strongly say so. A pause. Well, yes, the ones who are possessed usually speak not in English but in their own native dialect.

The next day, after phoning Sr Cosmas, I went to see Fr David and elicit his help. A wonderful, experienced, holy and kindly priest. He welcomed me as a messenger from the Holy Spirit because 'now is the appointed time'. He had been wanting to come to the school and was hoping the school would approach him, as he did not want to be seen as imposing. We would have a prayer meeting in which he would inform the girls that the powers of grace were far stronger than any an evil spirit could wield. Of course, most of the cases were self-induced, or a result of over-heated imaginations fed by horror movies, but witchcraft and evil spirits were part of the culture and, in the past, many of their ancestors had, indeed, made pacts with the devil. Unlike in the West, evil spirits do not have to go in disguise. This is the front line, and the Dominations and Principalities and forces of evil do not have to hide.

His compassion for the girls was evident, for the strain they are under, very many needing counselling because of domestic problems. Many children of polygamous marriages, with stepmothers who were uncaring and unloving, made their lives, their young lives, pits of sadness and worry. They needed guidance, counselling, gentleness and love.

What a priest!

The next day, thirty or so MPs visited the school. After all the formalities, the meal, the speeches, the hotly contested debates (the school was the venue, not the matter of discussion), as evening came swiftly down, the school fields were littered with the usual scattering of 'Little Bernadettes': young girls like pictures of Bernadette of Lourdes, completely oblivious to the important visitors, unselfconsciously, sincerely kneeling on the grass and praying fervently as though it were the most natural thing in the world. Some, I hear, even fast. But every night, in whichever part of the field they are in, they will kneel and pray. What faith. A sort of miracle.

17.10.2004 Highs and Lows

It's the sudden jolt; the brain out of control, no longer the computer processing and monitoring everything going on; the instinctive grabbing of the bedpost as the bed whirls around, spinning, rising, falling, at an incredible speed; the palpitations and the gasping for air, and the awful, inevitable, inexorable lurching towards violent vomiting, the washes of perspiration pumping out and the sheer physical feeling of helplessness and loss of control, subject to the whims of a malign force within you. Weak as a kitten indeed. It was one of the worst cases of vertigo I had had in years. And on this, the night before the final preparation for Independence Day.

Crowe lay all day, not even able to move his head from side to side, never mind up, in case it launched another go on the spinning wheel. Crowe was precariously close to feeling sorry for himself before using the magic mantra – Darfur – which puts all petty inconveniences into perspective.

And yet, the day launched itself into a sky of kindness. Kristin, from the American Peace Corp, who visits and stays with us once a week, going to Mbale to get money from her bank because I couldn't – a journey entailing not only travelling eighteen miles, but queuing for ever at the bank (the English think they are queuers; hah, amateurs) – and shopping for us. Betty, the head, going to three pharmacists before finding the one with the correct tablets. And the stream of children, knocking and enquiring after and sending concerned good wishes for 'Mr Patrick'. Lads, lads, lads. It's easier to handle anything else than kindness. If the vertigo left me weak, the kindness nearly killed me.

And then... Saturday, the next day. I could put my feet to the floor without retching or falling, and would take it easy and show my face at the celebrations of Independence Day. Wow. And again I say: wow. Wow, wow, wow, WOW. What celebrations.

In the packed hall, the girls giggling, gleeful, shifting, gasping with suppressed – but not too suppressed – excitement, and then the show.

An astonishing traditional tribal dance from the north, the girls playing both male and female parts for this courtship dance, dressed up, white faces (boys) and leaves in their hair, playing – oh, such rhythm – of the drums, and the exuberant, abandoned but controlled dancing, lasting all of fifteen minutes. Energy. Joy. Power. A great pride in expressing and exhibiting their traditional, wonderful and deeply loved dance, knowing instinctively how powerful and richly beautiful and proud it was. Wow!

At the end of the dance, the leader comes and receives a *cadeau*, a gift from the guest of honour, and takes it with the air of one fully entitled to it for her troupe (this from a usually very diffident group), with a sort of pride, and how rightly so. And oh, yes: whilst the drum beat out its pulsating, complex, compulsive rhythm, all the time, the leader, still dancing throughout, blew a whistle! I would never have thought a whistle could have such an effect. I think it is the first time I have heard it used as a musical instrument. And it adds an urgency and excitement to the whole wonderful madness.

We had, at intervals, two other traditional dances from different parts of Uganda; each distinct, very different, particular. I was unaware that the human body and its constituent parts could move in such different patterns, independent of each other, all at the same time! No wonder David danced before the Lord.

This was followed by the play (what I wrote), with two splendid songs by Anne, and the girls loved them. The theme was Ugandan Independence and was (I hope) mad and funny and well-received. One girl was the president of Uganda and brought the house down, and, of course, we had the presidents of France, Japan, Ireland, the Queen of England etc., and I did my piece for fostering good relations with the West by giving George W. the immortal lines:

> I've been near
> And I've been far
> And today I learnt that
> Uganda's in Africa.

Yep, somehow sums him up.

The afternoon was meal time (meat), followed by bull roast – each girl given a barbecue stick with three pieces of beef on it – pop and what should have been music, but the electricity was off and the generator broke down… so they made their own. Ah, the drums, the drums.

The next day, we had further celebrations because of the 'handover' from the outgoing Young Christian Students to the ones taking their roles next year. These girls are extraordinary. Prayer is not divorced from life, but is as natural as breathing. These girls have prayer meetings twice a week, visit the sick on the compound, keep the compound tidy and, from their meagre resources, send aid to the children in the war-torn country of the north. Yes, I know. You bow your head.

Let me finish with quoting a poem a fourteen/fifteen-year-old wrote and recited to a packed hall of fellow students, who received the poem in such a positive and appreciative manner. It wasn't seen as uncool or smarmy or whatever, but as an expression of how they all perceive the situation.

Education

Education, Education.
Education is like an orange
Hanging from a tree,
Situated in the desert
Along a traveller's path.
I am a traveller.
A traveller?
Yes, a traveller.
And I am hungry and thirsty
But the tree is so high.
So high.
Yes, so high
I need a ladder.
The ladder is St Clare's High School.
The teachers are my strivers,
Striving and reaching for the fruit.
Yes, education is like an orange.
Parents buy it for me.

23.10.2004 Portraits

Mary

Sweet Mary, found quietly sobbing in the corridor. Earnest and dying for education. Her father has died of AIDS; his family came, as is the African custom, and purloined everything, leaving his widow with nothing, utterly destitute. Mary, without a father, without hope.

Some Christian group might give her help if she can prove she has attended school. She came to ask for her school report. I had only met her that morning but was reluctant to let her go. I was assured that it would be all right. I made her promise she would let us know, and not to worry; something would be done. She disappeared.

Due to the generosity of people back home, we found her a sponsor. Happily, her uncle called in to school (he can barely support his own two children's fees) and promised he would get her to call. So far, two weeks later, we have heard nothing, and I worry. Please God, she'll get in touch.

I cannot resist letting one or two of the children tell their story in their own words. I could not match their natural eloquence and heartfelt feelings.

Anne gave them the title 'Mum' in an essay. These stories are true, and they capture the reality of their plight, their lives. I have had permission to publish the following extract.

Santa's story

> How caring she was! The most special woman in my life was Mum. I loved her so much I don't think I can live without her in my life.
>
> It was my birthday party when I realised Mum would do anything on Earth for me. 'Mummy,' I called. 'Yes, dear,' she answered me very fast and came into the house.

I thought she was going to refuse my request. I told her about my preparations for the birthday party and she promised she would make it a colourful one for me.

As the days went by she told me to start designing the welcome cards. I was so happy but I wasn't sure she would help me best.

The next morning she asked me to give her a push to the bank to withdraw some money. I was filled with joy and happiness because I knew my deal was getting through. I accepted, dressed up, and went with her.

On that evening we went around shopping for the party. She bought me everything I asked for. What a lovely mother God gave me. My birthday party was very enjoyable and colourful. I received very many gifts from my best friends. The next day everybody talked about my party and commented on how beautiful and outstanding it was.

All this happened because of my caring and loving mum. She would always make me feel so happy. Mum cared for me and always gave me comfort when I was sick. She made sure I was one of the happiest children in the school. I also made sure I never made her angry because I wished never to make her upset because of me. Since my mum passed away, I don't think I will ever get a wonderful, beautiful, caring and loving mum anywhere else in this world. I will live to remember Mummy.

My fellow students always praised her and wished they had a mum like mine. I always felt proud of her and felt good when people talked about her good helping work. If there was anyone to leave you alone on Earth, Mum would never even think about it. Even if your father wanted to do without you, your mum will always plead for you. It is very special to live with Mum, and hard to forget her. Nothing and no one is better than your mum. God gives and takes away. Pray that he does not take your mum.

23.10.2004 Blow Winds and Crack Your Cheeks

My A level students. Was there ever a more pleasant, compliant, co-operative, lovely class in the whole history of pedagogy or education? English Literature, and I stress English; *Jane Eyre, King Lear, A Man for All Seasons. A Man for All Seasons*! For heaven's sake, they don't even know what a season is! How English can you get? Yep, one of my all-time favourites, but c'mon, *King Lear*?

But the girls: committed, demure, hungry for knowledge, polite. Now don't get me wrong; these girls have their faults, and one day I'll find them. These exuberant, lively, convivial girls are transformed as they enter the classroom, losing all spontaneity, becoming merely receptacles of knowledge. My style is more engaging, lively, interactive. So we started to act out *Lear*: giving them parts; making them speak out loud, stand up, walk around. I frightened the holy Moses out of them at one stage by bellowing out the 'blow winds and crack your cheeks' speech. Then they had to bellow it out. Great fun.

That very night, we had the mother and father of a tropical storm; nothing held back, no holds barred, a real hell-for-leather take-that-in-the-eye storm. The next morning, I met them and, eyes gleaming with excitement, they said, 'Last night, *King Lear*.'

Later on that day, crossing the field, I could hear them shouting, 'Blow winds and crack your cheeks,' and then breaking out into peals of laughter. And people wonder why you teach.

23.10.2004 *The Bank*

It was a series of minor mishaps that singly would not have disturbed the skin of your custard, but taken together could lead to an upset stomach, or at least the use of intemperate language. Or, as my old granny would say, 'Bollix'.

There is one cash machine that will take our credit cards in Mbale. On our weekly visit to the great Metropolis, it broke down. We borrowed money and scraped by. The next week, bedridden, electricity off, water taps not functioning and penniless, you felt the good Lord trying out his wicked sense of humour, or trying to make a point.

This spurred me on to open an account. Ah, yes. Are banks the same the whole world over? It does give you a small insight into the plight of 90% of our fellow human beings. Banks are smart, official, symbols of wealth and power, a law unto themselves. Everything, the unhurried pace of work, the queues, the lights, the shiny desks, the computers, the phones, the casual indifference towards the customer, the air of tranquillity, the boredom of the tellers, everything screams silently at you that they are in control and you must obey. No wonder people rob them.

BANKER: Yes, you have the letter that we asked for last week confirming that you work at St Clare's High School... but it does not state that you reside there.

ME: But it does on my identity card.

BANKER: Please arrange for the letter to state your place of residence... Thank you. Please fill this form and return it with a reference from a customer from the bank.

ME: But I have only just arrived and no one at the school has an account.

BANKER: Please. Get a reference.

My passport, letter, reference from a customer I blackmailed and mugged are duly submitted (and by that time I have almost submitted under the weight of bureaucracy). But you must deposit money in order to open an account. The money – my money – is locked in the machine. For two weeks it hasn't worked.

Card in; card out. Card in; card out.

ME: The machine isn't working.

A slow turn of the head.

BANKER: Yes, it is.

Card rejected.

ME: The machine isn't working.

BANKER: Yes. Communication problem. Keep trying. It will. Be patient. *A smile.*

Reflection

Poverty and power. To experience, even for a moment, life without money, or access to money, illustrates the panic, the helplessness and frustration of being locked out: of peering into the shop window of the world, knowing you have no right to be there, to be part of it; you can only observe and watch. Poverty equals powerlessness.

We are here for the sole purpose of 'empowering' these girls, of enabling them to have control over their lives, to make decisions for themselves, to shape their own destiny. But, as long as we allow poverty to distort that destiny, the fight will be all the harder. We have, however, no other choice but to attempt to give them the tools whereby they have access to power, to control.

There are, thank God, some models of success and power; the lovely lady from Kenya who last week won the Nobel Peace Prize for her environmental work is a shining light. I have not got the insight of the inestimable Karl Marx, but you need not be a genius to see that our system of wealth and, more to the point, wealth distribution is plain bonkers.

The poor we have always with us; but surely that does not mean to the point of extinction, of degradation, or of annihilation through disease, despair and death. Ahhh! Sometimes the only response is anger and fury.

29.10.2004 Food, Glorious Food

There is food, and there is food. There is food you consume to keep alive; you ask nothing more of it. Unexciting, edible, maybe even unpalatable. But it does its job and it is food. Then there is FOOD. Food you relish, enjoy, savour; food that you taste before, after and during the meal; food that delights the eye, sings to your ear, entices the juices, seduces the senses, brings the appetite to a crescendo of anticipation, conquers all resistance and drowns you in pleasure. Yes. Food.

Nowadays, I fantasise about chicken breasts, legs of lamb, tenderloin of pork, *bœuf bourguignonne*, balti lamb, sausages 'n' mash, bacon 'n' egg, pasta sauces, casseroles in Guinness, chicken in wine. Ahh, yes.

What has saved us from complete insanity and starvation is the roast potato. Anne has fallen in love with the roast potato, the chilli roast potato. Or, as they call it over here, the Irish potato. There are sweet potatoes and Irish potatoes. Not South American potatoes, not English or British or French or any other country potatoes, just Irish potatoes. Who says the missionaries came here?

We have a broken old gas cooker, retrieved from the Titanic, I think, which has three working gas jets, and we have bought a small portable electric oven. When the electricity works (hah!) we do casserole – famine-starved chicken and vegetable casserole – and, nearly every night, roast potatoes.

Sometimes, we simple country rural folk talk about going up to Sin City, known as Kampala, which has night life and enticing decadent hedonistic things like... cheese, and wine, and edible cuts of meat, and restaurants and pizzas and IRISH PUBS... fantasies, fantasies. We rarely get there, but in your dreams, the taste... pass the water, I'll do without the bread.

Did you know...?

I'm getting jungle fever. Strange thoughts enter my head.

I now do yoga. Well, 'do yoga'. It's like saying I've bought a racket and therefore I'm a tennis player. Or I've read the biography of Hillary and therefore I'm a mountain climber. And, to carry the mountaineering metaphor on a little, I'm starting out to reach the foothills of the mountain called yoga.

Anyway, one of the exercises requires you to lie on your back and shoot your legs up into the air with your arms supporting the small of your back, resting on your shoulders. You look straight up and all you can see are your legs, your feet and the ceiling. If you look at your knees in this meditative position, they look (I swear) just like smiling dolphins. They do. Honest. Try it... go on, try it and see.

Jungle fever, jungle fever, jungle fever...

Marking some work the other day, I came across a sentence that could be written nowhere else and will live with me forever:

'As long as the sun is over my mango-shaped head, I will live to recall this day come rain or come shine.'

Wow!

Feminism

Since coming here, I have become an avowed feminist. When I read what our girls have to contend with: domestic violence, traditional subjugation of wives, denigration and defilement of young girls... move over, Germaine Greer; you're not radical enough!

Question:

When I came here, I thought my mind would be filled with noble thoughts, I'd be a new me. Why, oh, why do I still find myself ignoring what is around me, the sun, the scenery, the greenery, the sky, the trees, the vegetation, the landscape, and find myself preoccupied with and fretting about trivia?

Life is life. Whether in Budaka or Bulkington, Kampala or Coventry.

We should heed the words of Teresa of Avila:

Let nothing disturb you, let nothing frighten you; all things are passing.

If only.

29.10.2004 The Rosary

Every night, between forty and fifty come to our house and, on the grass or on the veranda, kneel and recite the rosary, and then sing a hymn. They are the Young Christian Society. They kneel and, in their unselfconscious way, pray with simplicity, sincerity and fervour. And they do the whole rosary, including the credo at the beginning. Two little boys from the village sometimes sneak in, and when they spy the girls kneeling, from about thirty yards out, they kneel!

Afterwards, they sing a hymn. My favourite I shall set down. They sing it as a love song, meaning every word.

Darling Jesus

> Darling Jesus,
> Darling Jesus,
> Oh, my darling Jesus,
> You are a wonderful Lord.
>
> I love you so much,
> Darling Jesus,
> Oh, my darling Jesus,
> You are a wonderful Lord.
>
> The most excellent is Jesus,
> Shout alleluia amen,
> The most excellent is Jesus,
> Shout alleluia amen.
> Alleluia.

They sing it with such natural joy and fervour. He is their darling, as they are his. Their faith is intimate, immediate, personal and emotional. It contrasts starkly with mine: scholastic, over-intellectual, sceptical, cautious, a weak withered plant next to their luxuriant growth. It is time I took my bucket to their well.

10.11.2004 The Darker Side

After the celebratory Mass, I went to see Sr Kevin, the wonderful head of the primary school, kind, kindly and motherly. Looking around as I waited in her office, I glanced at the large posters decorating her wall. Standard issue, I suspect, from the ministry of education, exhorting parents to strive to be good guardians with sentiments like 'Don't make your child carry heavy loads – it stunts their growth', 'Don't shout and argue in front of the children, it harms them' and then one with two people leading off a child, saying 'Don't sacrifice your child!', presumably on the grounds that it stunts their growth. A wee bit over-the-top.

The next day, I read in the paper that two men had been arrested, thwarted in their attempt at sacrificing a seven-year-old whom they had abducted. This led to my enquiring into such practices and, to my growing alarm and horror, realising that, far from being a unique case, it was not, indeed, an uncommon occurrence. Many children are sacrificed, especially in the bush. The hold that witch doctors have over remote country villages is awesome, and placating the spirits may involve their sacrificing not just a child but a child or children they love. Or it may be to bless a new building by burying a child in the foundations Apparently, parents were on red alert in Kampala a few years ago, when a spate of new buildings were being erected!

When you get over the initial incredulity, you ask why. Why or how could anyone do it? Fear and power. The people feel powerless, are powerless in the hands of angry gods or spirits, or fate, and life is cheap and brutal and precarious. Anything that will lighten the load, placate these gods, give them some measure of solace and control, is to be grabbed. No, of course it does not in any way condone this repulsive and heinous barbarity, but you can see what drives people to such madness. Who are they to gainsay the man with secret knowledge and power?

Nor can we in the West, at our sophisticated dinner parties, afford to raise a quizzical eyebrow and murmur about savage practices, when we have our own: the multiplicity of paedophile rings; the hordes of poor sex slaves smuggled in from the East; the blithe millions of late abortions when babies are butchered inside the womb to facilitate their extraction, a practice as barbarous and savage and gory as any here.

Child sacrifice. Here, it is done in the vain hope of achieving favours or power or release; it is not done to achieve mere convenience.

Sometimes, it strikes you that we live in a mad world, with no sense of values, little to cling to. Evil is evil, whether it is camouflaged or disguised or in the open, and often it seems to – no, does – triumph. We are fighting dominions and powers. Let us cling to the light.

10.11.2004 Exasperation and Exultation

Mass was to begin at 9.30 a.m., only the PP had forgotten to mention it might not begin till 10 a.m.

Our girls waited patiently and, at 9.55 a.m., they began to sing hymns to keep themselves occupied. The Mass, African time, began at 10.15 a.m. It finished at 12 p.m.

I tried to struggle against my Western impatience; tried to be calm, to use the time for prayer, to rise above my rising ire, to accept graciously the pace of African life. But oh, it's difficult. It's like sitting in a traffic jam: if someone told you exactly how long it would be, you would accommodate yourself to that length of time, but it is the not knowing, the uncertainty that raises the blood pressure and exasperates. On top of this, the Africans, or at least the Ugandans, have in spades the gift of the gab. In any meeting, everyone has to speak at length, even if they are repeating what everyone else has said. And the sermons; if they don't preach for half an hour, the people haven't had their money's worth. They reckon 'why take five minutes when you can take an hour?'!

All of this is true, to my shame. And yet, what a magnificent Mass; what a brilliant occasion! There was a special blessing Mass for those children completing their primary education. It involved the priest laying hands on every child, whilst we, since we belong to the priesthood of Christ and can therefore bless, held our hands over them. Beautiful. I know how Moses felt.

The exultation. The primary school prepared the Mass, read the readings, made the speeches, led the prayers of the faithful (all 500 of them) in their own language, and sang. And they were magnificent. They read clearly, intelligently, joyously. Wonderful. Well worth the wait!

10.11.2004 Travelling Light

I am an old contender. I was brought up facing the rigours and running the gauntlet of the London Underground. No rookie me. I know what it's like to be in a packed train, unable to open a newspaper for lack of space, and developing the eerie capacity of being able to ignore and blank out the person who is in such close proximity that you can count their nasal hairs or indulge inadvertently in Eskimo snogging. I know. I know.

But that is a relatively short journey; a blink; a jot; endurable. And then there is the African taxi, or the Ugandan taxi: a vehicle like a minibus, which probably saw service with Rommel in the desert and which is supposed to have a maximum of fourteen passengers but carries up to twenty. The more passengers, the more profit.

'Intimate' is the word. When you are sitting next to someone whose kneecaps, thighs, hipbones are joined to yours, and your arm is round the back of their neck because that's the only place it will go, you achieve a kind of intimacy you haven't enjoyed with your closest family or friends in your life. Indeed, the last time I approximated towards such intimacy, our youngest child was born. And it lasts forever – or four hours, anyway. On top of which, if you don't shift your feet occasionally, the hens that are under the back seat will peck you. And your genial companion sitting on, next to or over you will inform you that, with such greenery and such a climate, you are living in paradise. It would be impolite to demur, or to venture that on occasion it is a little hot and humid. Instead, you smile and agree. 'Yes,' he says. 'Paradise. Except for the poverty.'

And, you add to yourself, the lack of electricity, the Keystone Kops, traffic, the helter-skelter life-threatening boda-bodas, snakes and mosquitoes. But yes: paradise.

Got locked out of the convent later that night – but that's another story!

10.11.2004 The Birth of the Blues

Night time. Searchlights in place. Machine guns loaded. Net firmly in place covering the bed; not one scintilla of space between the bed and the net by which a cunning mozzie may to enter. C'mon, mozzies, do your worst.

2 a.m. in the darkest night, a voice calling: 'Hello. Hello.' Get up, get dressed in a fashion (not fashionably), go to front door and find there is an emergency. One of the staff has gone into labour.

The solution is obvious, even to me. Get the school truck. No key. No driver.

Phone the driver.
Phone off.
Phone the police.
'Hello. What do you want?'
'This is St Clare's School, round the corner. We need an ambulance, or at least a taxi. One of the staff has gone into labour.'
'Brother, please put the phone down.'
Click.
Phone the police again
'We only have one vehicle, which is for accidents.'
'But the woman is in labour. We need to get her to hospital.'
Click.
Phone hospital. No ambulance. Give taxi number. Taxi driver says no, he's going to sleep. Everyone has their phone switched off; the priest, the head, everyone.

In desperation, phone Sr Leah. Yes, she had gone to sleep, but her guardian angel has woken her up and she will gladly loan the vehicle. Just walk up to her place.

We accompany the lady to the high road (the great and wonderful young teacher Dominic getting the driver and coming to the rescue). Dominic and the lady teachers stay, whilst I, the driver of Sister's truck and his friend set off up the beaten old track of a road to Sister's. It's a long road. In the dark, African dark, it's a very long road. We set out armed with a torch, quickly, resolutely, and out of your mind go mozzies, snakes, army ants, wild animals or thieves. Just get there, rescue the girl.

We arrive. Leah is there, and her sister colleague, who is a midwife and who has a small maternity place there (no one at the school knew!). Bring the girl here.

Relief and cheers all round.

The next day, she is transferred to the hospital and gives birth by a caesarean operation. Joy and wonder.

That night, you go to bed and all you can see are mozzies, snakes, soldier ants, wild animals…

28.11.2004 Heads and Tales

Maggots. It was the maggots that did it for him. The baby, less than a day old, had been lifted from an open latrine. There was little, if any, hope. The arms had no circulation; the umbilical cord was six inches long. The little mite was in such a filthy state, covered with excrement, that the overwhelming putrid stench induced an almost impossible-to-resist urge to vomit violently, to retch your guts up. On top of that, the little thing had cuts to his chest and lower abdomen. But it was the maggots crawling all over the thing he was wrapped up in, and, more appallingly, coming out of him, that were screamingly shocking.

The local hospital had sent him straight to the abandoned children's home. They had not washed him, cleansed him, examined him; just rejected him. The home reacted furiously, but Joe said, 'Forget that; look to the baby.' They took him immediately to the International Hospital. No hope, but they had to try, at least.

The hospital took the 'Rogers' child (probably named after the good soul who retrieved it), cleaned it, washed it, pumped it full of strong antibiotics and placed it carefully in an oxygen tent. And waited. And resigned itself.

It took two days for the maggots to finally be cleared from inside his little body. They just kept coming and coming. 'He was a man rejected by many.'

The home has seen many tragic cases. Not everyone is saved.

Two weeks later, another event. That was six weeks ago from now. Another baby arrives at the home; this time a beautiful boy, but accompanied by his mother, who held him so lovingly and tenderly, the staff were delighted. And then she said, 'I must have him. He's mine. How do I adopt?'

It was the little latrine boy. No one recognised him. The lady holding him was the chief nurse who had loved him back to life.

That thing, that abandoned rejected object, transformed into an object of love; a person adored, doted on, loved. She had nursed, prayed, coaxed and nurtured him back to life, and now wanted to hold him and hold onto him forever.

Oh, the baby has been given a new name. Ekyewunyo. Miracle baby.

28.11.2004 Village and Village Idiot

It is called a village, which is a pseudonym for a refugee camp. Language and names make a difference. But even in such a place hilarity can break through, though at the time it didn't seem hilarious.

A new young volunteer arrives. Welcomed warmly. The next day, this young, athletic idealist goes for her morning run. She starts running. So does the whole village – in panic. The only experience these villagers have of running is in fleeing, and you only run when you are fleeing from marauders or the army or murderers, running from rape or torture or death.

It took some time to restore calm and peace and understanding, followed by relief and laughter.

She's stopped running.

28.11.2004 From Arusha with Love

Mount Kilimanjaro – the early morning, just-past-dawn sun above the clouds lighting up the glory of the summit. It was breathtaking; it was the Psalms, Mount Olympus, Zeus and the Gods. It confirmed de Chadin's contention that every stone, every rock, every seemingly inert thing has a within as well as a without, an inner dimension. It was immutable, timeless, alive and, in its imperious way, didn't even notice this gnat of a plane buzzing by. It was not the only peak we would reach that week.

Capacity building and management of change was the official programme, but, with the assistance of our splendid facilitators, we adapted the programme. It was lively, interactive, hotly debated and passionate; hardly surprising when you consider the people involved. Each time I meet the VMs, I am deeply impressed with their energy, commitment, dedication and feistiness.

All of them wanted to talk about their projects; not because they were self-centred, but because they wanted to make sure they were doing the best for them. They were not uninterested in capacity building and change (the very stuff we are involved in), but they wanted to discuss the real-life challenges we face here and now. It was refreshing and, like the original training, exhilarating, invigorating and utterly exhausting! Wow!

The variety of personnel and personalities.

The two young girls, effervescent, streetwise, experienced and just out of childhood themselves (and if they ever heard I said that, I am dead), Helen and Nickie. Michael and Brian, in different regions, both looking after street children and working in slums, always in the shadow of danger and violence, who are never careless, always aware, take precautions but never let anything inhibit their work; 'ah, sure, if you thought about it all the time, you'd do nothing.' On asking one of them when they had been mugged, 'What did they get?' 'An elbow in the face.'

But all of them. Doctors, anaesthetists (Mary 'I'm a gasman'), professors, mechanics, teachers, accountants, administrators, project managers, social workers. People living in extreme circumstances, refugee camps, in remote harsh places. All committed to the VMM; all passionate, compassionate; all human, and the majority young. There are, of course, some on the other side of the hill, like us (notably Kevin, who is seventy and has been with the VMM forever – well, eleven years – and has seen it almost disappear only to see it rise, reinvigorated, reinvented, with a new vision and a new expansion of long-term commitment to their projects). Exciting times. Inspirational times.

When you get such a mixture, there are going to be differences of emphasis, differences of opinion about how to achieve our targets, but there is at heart a unity of purpose, a deep desire to serve, to develop and sustain, and a determination to be one with the poor and marginalised.

The group is like an orchestra, with virtuosi, brilliant soloists; with Vincent, the conductor; Joe, the leader of the orchestra; Ana, the road manager, making sure we arrive on time in the right place with the right music, co-ordinating the whole thing; Ben making sure we are fed, and John and Noreen smoothing our path and pampering us. And Alice and Celia – they are the VMM, but when the orchestra plays, there is something beautiful achieved, a harmony of heaven. And, amongst all those trumpets and pianos and oboes and brilliant violins, even our little triangle can be heard!

Another concert soon, please.

16.01.2005 The Returnees

Is it instinctive, do you think? Does this incredibly successful method form in the mind naturally, without prior knowledge or experience, or is there some Academy of Brutality and Cruelty that passes on this secret covert ritual, this satanic methodology that is at once able to both destroy the self and make it utterly obedient and dependent at the same time? Perhaps there is a terrorist school for training in these black arts, honing skills in these arcane and dangerous techniques? Perhaps it just surfaces naturally from the darkest recesses of the mind; a recalling from a common, tribal, barbaric memory from ancient, savage times. It is, indisputably, horribly and revoltingly effective.

When the children of nine upwards are abducted, the first thing one must do is destroy all ties with the past; one must, literally and metaphorically, cut off all blood and relationship ties with the old self and the former life. This is harshly but easily done, by making the children bludgeon or club to death one of their group. It may be their younger brother or sister, or a neighbour, or even their own mother. They will use machetes or clubs or whatever and beat them or hack them until they are dead. If they are boys of a certain age, they will be forced to gang rape a girl captive, be it their sister or whoever. Then they are 'trained': they are sent on forced marches; they are fired at with blank bullets to show that bullets don't hurt; they are sent on raids to steal from villages and kill the inhabitants; they are regularly abused physically and emotionally and, if girls, sexually. Certain girls are chosen as sex slaves for the officers. All of them face constant abuse and are drilled to the point of exhaustion, until they don't know who they are, or what they are, or who they were or where they came from. The only security they have, the only loyalty they have, the only relationship and safety they have is with the group. If they dare try to escape, they are killed or maimed horribly. It is a life of relentless horror; they are child soldiers.

It is difficult to absorb. It is medieval, gothic. It would tax the imagination of the most inventive writer of revengers' tragedies with the litany of bizarre and excessive tortures: gouging out of eyes; lopping off of limbs; disfigurement of features; chopping off someone's nose and face and making him eat them. It is the practice and image of living hell.

Some have escaped, some been released and some been rescued. What do you do with such damaged children? How do you recapture a destroyed or discarded childhood; an unfinished, half-formed self; a fledgling that was about to enter into independent selfhood, now distorted and misshapen? This is a being often with no relationships with anyone or anything, not even with themselves; with a memory that is kaleidoscopic and confused and non-functioning; with a stunted, emotionally crippled personality. The trauma is severe; so deep, one wonders if the emotional blood will ever be able to flow freely in their veins again.

There is to be a meeting in Lira on the 13–16 January to discuss the plight of the Returnees, and to see what can be done to secure their long-term care and rehabilitation. The dioceses of Gulu, Soriti and Lira are holding a combined meeting. The counselling and care offered has to be first class and has to be tailored to their particular needs; anything shallow or inappropriate could do more damage than good. We must look to other traumatised victims in other times throughout the world so that we can learn from them and not reinvent the wheel, but provide a service that can constructively nurture them back into reality and into relationships with themselves and with each other. As Caryl Houselander said, we must 'love' them back into reality.

It will need expert psychiatric and psychological counselling and healing, a lot of prayer and a lot of time. Perhaps then the Returnees may become the Resurrectees. We hope. We pray.

16.01.2005 *Reflections*

It is a curious, surrealistic experience to live with poverty but not in poverty: to breathe, smell, touch poverty; to be surrounded by it and watch its effects and yet be somehow distant from it! It defeats my powers of analysis, my powers of control or understanding.

Poverty and I are old friends. I am a product of the forties: a child of what is now known as a one-parent (widowed) family, and when I was nine my mother and I became what are now referred to as economic migrants. Yes, I remember bare feet (not, I hasten to add, my bare feet; I remember no deprivation or want), rags, beggars, grim stark desperation, but I remember dear old Dublin as a place of life and humour and happiness and impromptu children's street concerts. But poverty was as endemic and natural as the Dub accent.

I know poverty. Since then, I have known poorish times, times of scarcity and a little anxiety. As a young teacher, along with countless others, I had to undertake what is most inappropriately known as 'moonlighting', which sounds fairly romantic, but which in reality leaves you exhausted, worn out and totally knackered for your real job. For years, the long summer holiday was an opportunity to get a job on a building site so we could grab a bed and breakfast beach holiday. And the crisis when the kids needed new shoes! (What did they do to the last pair? Oh, very nice; they wore them. Wore them bloody out!) But that is not poverty.

Poverty is a cancer; a disease; an all-embracing, suffocating, paralysing disease. It makes you impotent, debilitated, unable to act. It robs you of your dignity and humanity. On one level, the deepest level, it forces you to watch your child die, as you have no money to pay for the malaria treatment. It leaves you helpless as your wife loses her newborn, or not born, because there is no money to deal with complications. It makes you witness your child descend into the nightmarish life of the streets because there is no other choice. These are cases that occur every day.

Yet here is a country of rich laughter. A country in which there is great, huge delight and love of everyday things. They cope, in spite of the constant presence of poverty, because they have a most wonderful capacity to live in the present, the now. Every day will give some little, eagerly accepted small delight, which they share with their friends. Whatever small grace is bestowed, it is graciously, joyously received. This attitude is reflected by the astounding fact that some local languages do not have a future tense. The future is not real. We could learn much from that attitude.

Those lucky enough to have a job constantly rob Peter to pay Paul, constantly dip into next month's pitiful salary to pay this month's bills. It is a scenario to induce nervous breakdowns. Yet it doesn't. School fees are an ever-present source of worry and anxiety, but people live from day to day. It leaves one humbled and aghast.

But it also leaves one seething with rage. If one supper or dinner is the epitome of living and generosity and the secret of life, it is surely the Last Supper, when the Lord poured out everything that he had: himself. The antithesis of that was the obscene fundraising dinner, when George Bush uttered those now-infamous words of 'the haves and have mores'. It enrages one to think that that is how we have chosen to organise the world. Let there be no mistake: this is the politics of envy. Not envy of their several houses and fancy yachts; let them keep their toys. But it is envy of their access to medicine, to clean water, to housing and shelter; of their never having to think about food or its lack, or worry about the well-being of their children.

There are the haves and have mores, and there are the haves and have nothings.

16.01.2005 *Christmas Scenes*

Christmas in a convent: images of prayer, softly sung hymns, wax, silence, incense. Yes, there was all that. And so much more. Such unmitigated fun. These little Cinderellas may not have gone to the ball, but boy, did they have a ball!

After the first Mass of Christmas came the excitement of opening presents; the glass of wine; mince pies and cakes; the wee wee dram of Jameson provided by me; the dancing to Bony M's 'Mary's Boy Child Jesus Christ'; the singing of songs, songs Irish, Scottish, English, whatever; gigging and giggling; innocent, girlish delight. These ladies of vast experience, each rich in their individuality, who hold in their faces years of shared suffering and pain and hope, rejoicing in the birth of their Saviour.

On Christmas day, we had the Christmas lunch, prepared by two of us. There was the usual anxiety for the turkey to turn out right, and the stuffing to be moist, and the roast spuds crisp, and as usual all was well and the feast good, and the wine warm, and the banter and stories well told and received. Great. The next day, or rather in the middle of the night, I received a present of malaria, but if you are going to get malaria, make sure you are in a convent; the treatment is second to none – or perhaps that should be second to nun!

Two days later, we are invited to join their sister convent in Jinja, where a very small community of two run a project. Our three nuns and two warm, urbane, missionary priests join us, along with a visiting VM colleague and dear friend, and again the banter, the food, the conviviality were excellent. This time, Anne decided to take advantage of our host's hospitality, and she came down with malaria. She stayed the night (two nights, in fact) in the convent, and the two splendid sisters nursed her and looked after her superbly. I was once again struck by their matter-of-fact deep spirituality. On the way to the medical centre, quietly praying and invoking the saints' prayers for protection: St Francis,

Our Lady, St Clare and, because the driver was a Muslim, Prophet Mohammed pray for us, to which the driver uttered a fervent 'amen'. Wonderful.

Recovered and well, we return home. Yesterday, the computer technician turns up to service our computers, and, as the way here with many, greets me as the prodigal son or a long-lost brother he hasn't seen for years, pumping my hand with twenty firm handshakes, grinning and jumping and wishing me long life and happiness. Yes, I know it may be a bit of salesmanship, but I don't think so. The guy is of such a happy disposition; it is his nature. The last and first time we met, I had my only in-depth political conversation since I got here. He was interested in everything. He wanted to know what the UK thought of Museveni, of Uganda, of the war in the north, of the corruption, of the poverty, of AIDS and unemployment. I hadn't the heart to tell him they don't think of them at all. He also wanted to know what we thought of Africa generally, and what we thought of Nelson Mandela. Here, at last, I could wax eloquent and say he was regarded as a world statesman; yes, on par with Churchill and Bill Clinton. And was Napoleon a great leader? Wow. I told him the Beethoven story of Eroica, but that indeed he was a great general; that he had huge leadership qualities, but was sadly flawed. Why didn't I study my European history more assiduously?

Today, however, after the initial greeting, I asked how the New Year had gone. His face clouded. How can anyone's New Year be anything but dreadful after the terrible tragedy of the tsunami disaster? It was shocking, and everyone must be affected. I was affected by his reaction and his empathy.

The whole event has shaken my faith to the core. There are just so many contradictions. I heard the most crass and banal and insensitive sermon on Sunday, by a priest who still carries within him a nineteenth-century theology, because it didn't matter, the only thing that matters is the next life, not this! As though our incarnation went for nothing. If this life doesn't matter, why have it at all? Are we not born for a purpose: to establish God's Kingdom on Earth? Are we not to build, here and now, a kingdom of peace and justice and love and community, and establish a world united in service?

Why did our loving Father, the source of our being, the giver of life, not intervene? We have the Pope telling us that Our Lady intervened in his attempted assassination by guiding the bullet. Maybe. Everyone is entitled to his belief. He didn't mention the fact that he was near a hospital, where there was on hand a team of expert doctors and surgeons. Perhaps there was heavenly intervention. But then you are forced to ask: is the Pope more important than hundreds of thousands of children? This mission we are embarked on here is as much a spiritual quest as anything else, and I am deeply perturbed by these events and the awful, wretched, evil war in the north. What is the answer? It is a mystery beyond my grasp. Somehow, somewhere, the answer lies in prayer. Somehow, our omnipotent God becomes, makes himself impotent, depending on our intervention through our desiring and asking for his help. But it is all too hazy, too unclear. I am still overwhelmed and lost.

The one ray of hope has been the world response. Even the arch-enemy, Bush, seems to be responding. The American people, as are the rest of the world, are most generous. Let's hope he institutionalises it, signs the Kyoto agreement, tackles free trade, controls globalisation, stops the patenting of every known and unknown plant and medicine in the world, and starts thinking globally.

Curiously, this morning's antiphon was, 'Many waters cannot quench love, neither can floods drown it.'

Mmmmmmmmmmm!

21.02.2005 *Gulu*

Gulu. Perhaps it should be known as Gulag. It is a war zone, and I have become a war correspondent.

The most striking and disturbing sight on reaching Gulu is the commuters. We were staying in the seminary about five kilometres outside Gulu. It was evening, and, as we drove in, it was like watching a Second World War newsreel; streams and streams of people were pouring into Gulu, of all ages, from little dots of four and five up to old men and women. They walked in single file, passively, listlessly, grimly. They seek the protection of the town, driven by fear of being raped or maimed or mutilated or butchered or abducted. There are thousands of them, and they sleep on verandas, on the hospital floors, in shop doorways and in makeshift shelters. The name 'commuter' belies their predicament; it makes it sound normal, or acceptable, but this fear has made them take this trek every morning and every night for the last eighteen years. For many of the children and teenagers, it is normal; it is all they have ever known. What does that do to family life?

The seminary we were lodged in and where the workshop took place is, as stated, about five kilometres outside the town. It has not been untouched by this terrible war. Two years ago, in the middle of the night, they woke up to pandemonium: torches, loud whistles, shouts and gunfire. One of the workers' children, an eight-year-old boy, wandered out on hearing the mayhem and was immediately shot dead. The Lord's Resistance Army raided one of the dormitories where the minor seminarians were lodged and abducted forty-one of them. To date, eleven are still missing, whether alive or dead is unknown, and thirty escaped or were released. It has left its scars.

The rector, a large, charismatic, passionate man, is also very brave. He had been in the bush the week before, with some high-level government and religious leaders, trying to broker a peace deal. In order to meet these people, you had to screw your courage up, because these people are capable of anything and there are never guarantees that you will be safe. In the event, all went well. But the rector was willing to take that risk, so passionate is he in seeking peace, so distraught at seeing his people being destroyed and his culture being eroded to the point of extinction. The land and the people are dying.

The shocking truth is that 800,000 people, 80% of the people in that district, are in camps. They are IDP camps: 'Internally Displaced Persons'. And even the term 'camp' fails to do justice to the horror that they are. They are not well-ordered holiday camps; they are areas onto which people have moved, like travellers at home, and built makeshift shelters. There is often a lack of proper facilities, like clean water or proper sewerage. The people's cattle have gone; their land has been abandoned and left untended; their homes are destroyed and their lives in disarray. Inevitably, with no work, little purpose or occupation, despair settles on the camps, and many take refuge in alcoholism. The women, as usual, are left to try to pick up the pieces.

These camps vary in size from 10,000 to 30,000. We were with one guy who worked in a camp with 67,000. And that is in that district. The priest from the next district told me they had over seventy such camps. The horror is hard to envisage, the ravages of this war to annotate; it has been raging for eighteen years. It is worse than that horror, the tsunami; in fact, it is a tsunami, a mind and heart and physical tsunami, an eruption that fractures and breaks individuals and families and communities, leaving them emotionally, psychologically and often physically wrecks. And the government are seen not always as the solution but as part of the problem; the army seen not always as an army of liberation but as an army of occupation, composed of soldiers from other parts of the country and other tribes not sympathetic to the people of Acholi. And the government does nothing for the displaced persons. The World Food Programme is the organisation that tries to feed them, and the voluntary sector tries to give them support. Indeed, some MPs wanted the president to declare the area a disaster area so that it could receive international aid and relief, but he refused.

I have been the eyes and ears of the VMM. It is too dangerous for our volunteers to venture into the area now, but, when peace does come, there will be a huge need for counsellors, child workers, social workers, family workers, nurses, doctors, teachers and whoever. Indeed, the seminary I stayed at is desperately short of Maths and Language teachers. The wonderful Fr Cyprian tried to persuade me I could commute to Gulu for two days a week. He was joking, but they are desperate.

There is, however, one thing we can all do now: we can pray, pray and pray.

Again. Pray for Our Lady, Queen of Peace, to shine her light on that dark and forsaken land, and to pour out her love and solace and bring these children relief and release.

30.01.2005 Give Us a Break: Breaking the Chains of Poverty and Oppression

The VMM are a voluntary missionary organization. We don't go round converting people; our mission is to witness and to serve the poor, the oppressed and the marginalised. We are development workers, working with our partners to empower them and assist them in their fight to win freedom from indignity, poverty and disease.

We have a host of projects all over East Africa and South America. We are to be found working in hospitals, schools, refugee camps, slums and famine-stricken outposts. We work with handicapped children, street children and abandoned babies, and, indeed, wherever there is a need or a call. Mainly we consist of young volunteers, but there are a few of a more mature (knackered) age, from all sorts of backgrounds and professions: carpenters, mechanics, nurses, electricians, doctors, accountants, social workers, teachers, pharmacists and project managers. Our call is to be in solidarity with the poor, and our main aim in all our projects is to ensure that, by the end of our project, we are redundant and have passed on the relevant skills to our local partners to enable them to take control, not only of the project, but of their lives and future.

We are in Uganda, a beautiful country. But it is a country riven and beset with all sorts of problems: crippling poverty, AIDS, diseases, unemployment and a terrible, horrific, savage and most bloody war.

We are far from that war where we are, but we face daunting problems and obstacles. St Clare's is a girls' school, and there's the rub: girls. Of all the groups in our society, girls are the most vulnerable. They are still an oppressed minority, still regarded as chattel, as commodities. They also face great poverty and a host of other difficulties. They are hungry for education, hungry for a way out, a way to break free from this cycle of poverty and depression.

We are the only girls' school in the whole area, and our avowed aim is to educate the girls, increase their skills base and, above all, to give them a sense of their own worth, to instil in them confidence and high self-esteem so that they can take their rightful place in society and help shape and fashion their and their country's future.

But there are difficulties. This is a poor country. For example, there is malaria. Malaria is endemic. A mosquito bites you and releases into your bloodstream thousands of parasites, which enter your blood vessels and attach themselves to your liver etc. If you are really unlucky, it is cerebral malaria, and that attacks your brain. If not treated, it is fatal. There is, as yet, no vaccine, because the big pharmaceutical companies do not find it lucrative or attractive. There are drugs that are effective and are cheap; but they are only cheap in our terms. The one or two euros it costs to get the drugs are beyond the means of countless people and, consequently, every day children die. Every day! Thousands every year. Life is cheap.

Our meagre fees – the school is a money-losing institute – go to pay the teachers' salaries and feed the children. The teachers earn, on average, about 110 euros a month. It is a boarding school, and the fees are about ten euros a week. Last year, sixty-three children had to leave because they could not meet the payment. That is the stark reality.

When we came, we were struck by two things: the attitude and hunger of the kids for education, and the appalling conditions in which they strive to learn. Make no mistake about it; the lady who founded the school is magnificent, and her aspirations noble, but it is costly. First of all, the loos. The latrines are in a very perilous state; one set are waiting for over a year to be drained, and the other set need wooden covers to prevent the descent of all the flies. They are outside and, in the dark, dangerous. There are two open cesspits that not only breed all sorts of contagious diseases but attract mosquitoes by the busload. If, in the dark, a child fell in, it would be the end of them. The dormitories are like long army barracks, with double metal bunk beds and not ONE fire door! Any outbreak of fire and ninety girls go up. No inside toilets, no inside washroom. The outside ones are laughably called 'showers', a euphemism if ever there was one, with no shower and no water. Every dormitory, like the classrooms, has broken windows, and most of the girls don't have nets, and this is the Mecca of mosquitoes. The laboratories have no equipment with which to do practical work; the library boasts of very few books; there are no globes for geography, no CD players for music, no instruments, and we learn computer theoretically (it's like learning to drive theoretically!). Each classroom has a blackboard and a piece of chalk; that is it.

But it is the emotional poverty that is the most devastating. Over here, they have a wonderful understanding of what death is. If a child loses one parent, she is an orphan; if she loses two, she is a full or complete orphan. Many of our girls are orphans. They face the further complication of polygamy, which is rife. Many hunger for affection, because a very real problem is the stepmother syndrome. Often, the second or third wife will be hostile towards the first wife's children. This is illustrated by the fact that, when parents come on parents' day (once a term), they are not allowed to bring food, a fact I found curious, but it is because of the practice of stepmothers poisoning their stepchildren.

There are other, more sinister forces at work, such as witchcraft, which is not relegated to the province of Hollywood horror movies, but which is a real and common danger. I could go on and on (I know I have done!), but suffice it to say we want these girls to be given a chance; to have a school that is safe, which is able to offer them a good education with proper basic equipment, which will offer them protection, counselling, guidance, which will nurture and foster them, which will heal their hurt and fill them with a sense of their own uniqueness and worth, and which will help them to realise they are God's precious ones, because they are.

30.01.2005 Bullets and Bikes

I am astonished by man's ingenuity. I am amazed and awestruck by the laws of physics and mathematics: that we can, by some internal combustion and explosion, hurtle tons of steel through the atmosphere and navigate this metal skyscraper onto the moon; I am left open-mouthed by the ability of gigantic, massive, overpowering, towering ships and tankers to purr their way around the globe. Wow! But the vehicle of all vehicles, the apogee, the summit, the mother and father of all inventions, the crème de la crème, must be the bike.

Of course, in the developing world, we have lorries and cars and coaches. We have coaches that defy, or try to, the law of gravity and time, that hurtle along at death-provoking speeds and belch out the most noxious and stinking black smoke; we have cars with tyres balder than me, and taxis that are held together by rust, but they are not what keeps the economy and the country running. That proud claim belongs to the bike.

There are thousands of bikes here. Everyone rides and owns a bike. Every granny, every kid, every macho man has their bike, and bikes in every conceivable condition. And when I say transport, I mean transport. What they carry on these bikes has to be seen to be believed: planks of wood five metres long, and narrow steel sheeting of the same dimension; boxes of eggs; racks of clothes; bedding and furniture; sacks of maize and sacks of cotton or sugar cane; anything! And if you consider their diet, which consists mainly of water, posho (a sort of maize-type porridge) and beans, or matoke (mashed unsweetened banana), they have the strength of a colossus. They can push and pull the world. They are a wonder of the universe. Where they get their strength from, God only knows. And the boda-boda guys could take on the strongest man competitors any time; no sweat. Or, perhaps, lots of sweat.

The bicycle keeps the economy and the country on the move.

It is the mechanism, the tool of the under-developed world. They need two things above all: water and a bike. With these two commodities, they conquer the world. They say here *'amazi warmee'*: 'water is life'. Indeed it is. Water is life, but having a bike is living!

The bike is ubiquitous; but equally so is the rifle. Every bank, every butcher, baker, candlestick maker, every shop that has more than two tins of beans on the shelf has an armed guard. They all look about fifteen.

And they use them. If the police are called out to a crime scene and spot the criminals (they are always referred to as 'thugs', even in the papers), they open fire! The paradox is that these most polite and welcoming and gentle of people turn savage if they catch a thief, or any ne'er-do-well. Mob violence and justice rule, and are meted out without mercy. But, if the thief gets away and their anger subsides, they forgive.

Bullets and bikes. What a great life!

13.02.2005 As I See It

Now that we've been here for a little while, six months, it is time to reflect on what the state of play is, what the challenges that confront us are, where we have come from and where we are going.

We are only really beginning to get our heads round the situation. What appeared on the surface to be just logistical problems turned out to have deeper roots: a history of relationships, power struggles, disunity, betrayal and distrust. There was also a conspiracy of silence, a feeling that, if all were said openly, we would, perhaps, walk away; or rather, I think, not so much that, but that if it were to be acknowledged openly, the whole enterprise might implode.

The school is very young, but has had a turbulent little history. A couple or three years ago, nearly all the staff (fourteen) were dismissed in one go. It is difficult to establish quite why, but it was an unhappy staff, with cliques; separate tribal groups; dissatisfaction; complaints; dereliction of duties, including not turning up to class. Some order was restored by that drastic action of dismissal.

The present head, very young and very inexperienced (but very canny and wise), had greatness thrust upon her. They did, before the year we came, appoint a deputy head who was, to put it bluntly, a disaster; she was not just not supportive to the head, but she was lazy and ineffective. She would not confront the students because she was afraid of them! These students, who would eat out of your hand if you asked them. There was also, in the staff room and at the termly staff meetings, an all-pervasive sense of disinterest, of *laissez-faire*, of disunity, or at least a lack of unity. Nothing was what it seemed. Everything was relegated to paper organisation, with not one thing happening in reality: no clubs, no counselling, no staff meetings, no accountability for teachers turning up to class or even teaching the syllabus. Worst of all, no respect for the head.

If I had known the situation, I may have handled the whole thing differently, but I am not sure it would have been as effective. Because I did not know the situation, I was outraged at the unprofessional attitude and behaviour of the staff, and I called a staff meeting. I'm afraid I hit the poor buggers like a bomb. When they attempted to display the same disrespect whilst I was speaking, by writing, or marking, or one even attempting to hold a conversation, I hit the roof; I told them to leave if they could not behave professionally, and that I would never show them that level of discourtesy! Yes, you could feel the atmosphere change, and, for a time, it was not comfortable. Now, of course, it is accepted how we behave.

It must be said, in their defence, that up to then they had never really been given a chance to air their concerns and grievances. They were now encouraged to do so. And they did.

Next, the head and I interviewed each member of staff in our house, in a relaxed atmosphere (non-threatening, with soda!), and each one was encouraged to give their own academic history, their vision for the future and their vision for the school. On top of that, we introduced a system whereby, if a teacher did miss a lesson or a duty, they had to report to me.

It has to be said, it was easy for me. I had been a head since Adam was a boy; I had been given the authority to carry out reforms (though it was never explained what reforms were necessary); they did not know me; I had the audacity and confidence from not being aware of the full scale of the problem, and, most importantly, I was a man! Isn't that a dreadful thing to have to say? Here, in an establishment that exists solely for the purpose of promoting girls!

Things are much better now. Most importantly, two key players, negative players, have gone; one, the deputy, of their own accord, thank God, and the other was pushed. Nothing to do with me, but the person had been a troublemaker and malcontent, and the opportunity came for the director to push.

We have appointed new staff. There is a completely different complexion, a different atmosphere in the staff room. At the beginning of term, we had a full day staff meeting. We spent the first part divided up into groups playing ice-breaking games (thank God for APSO training) and then, in those groups of three, devising the school mission statement. It took all morning, and at the end we had loads of statements. We took them away, and Anne reduced it all to one statement that captured the spirit of the staff; it shall be painted on the school entrance. There will be a fuller statement in our written journals, like our prospectus etc.

The next part of the day was taken over by the heads of departments, who were asked to sell their subjects to the rest of the staff. The subject leaders also gave their stories, and their ambitions for their subjects. It is then that your heart bleeds for them; to work under such circumstances, with little or no equipment, with inadequate resources, with a blackboard and a piece of chalk, is, to say the least, discouraging. We hope to change that.

The last thing we have done is secure two-year contracts. But those contracts also spell out exactly what the teachers' duties and responsibilities are, including the willingness to help run extra-curricular clubs and/or help in the girls' counselling. We shall meet the staff individually and witness their signatures. We are in the process of establishing a new school, a new culture, a new commitment. In our favour, the head in public, at staff meetings, is already much more confident. The past has been washed away. She has the opportunity to forge a new staff, a new school, a new vision.

The directors have to be congratulated for their ambition to establish a school to promote the place of girls and counterbalance the general trend, which does little to esteem or even recognise females. But their attitude is one of benevolent mill owners. They are not educationalists. They are astute, clever, but I do not think they understand the pre-eminence of teachers in creating a vibrant school. You have to have teachers who share the vision; who, indeed, create and make the vision. You must nurture them, cosset them, give them respect and motivation. For example, in the staffroom, not one chair; no plates; no lockers; nothing. They even threatened to take the staffroom away and use a small office. We now have plates and chairs (one each!) and even a cable TV! But in trying to establish that unity, that cohesiveness to achieve a common goal, there is a long way to go.

Relationships are the most important thing in a school, as anywhere. There is a conscious effort to set firm expectations in place regarding professional behaviour, but to banish timidity or fear, or the feeling of not being able to articulate your complaints or grievances. Openness and tolerance.

Challenges

The school is young and has many needs. This is not just for our stay, but for the VMM in future.

1 The lack of labs and equipment and resources. We hope to attract a grant to build three labs from the Irish government this year (God bless Ireland). We further hope to raise enough funds to buy textbooks etc. for the sciences, which are nationally seen as a priority over here, and which would give the girls a huge push up the social and employment, and therefore political, ladder. That department alone, if we bought all the textbooks they need and want, would cost over two thousand euros. We shall get some.

2 The dormitories are in bad need of refurbishment. Urgently we need fire doors (talk about dangerous). They are barracks. We need to build inside toilets and wash-rooms and put in pumped water, because it is just plain dangerous at the present: snakes and rape, which over here is not being alarmist. We also have to erect some partitions to give the girls some little privacy, inculcate a sense of their dignity and pride.

3 The library, now moved to a large, well-lit and airy room, has to become a central part of the school, well-stocked, much-used and open to all. It has to be attractive; tables, chairs, mats, curtains etc. We have appointed a librarian. But we need books, books, books.

4 Sports field and equipment. There is none. We have one uneven half-a-pitch, with a make-do volleyball net and an old netball set. No balls. The ones I bought last year have vanished(!). No other sports equipment is available. A good friend back home is sending me some. How vital for the all-round development is sports equipment.

5   All the other subjects need replenishing. A geography room. An arts room. Overhead projector.

6   The computer suite. Thanks to our benefactors back home, we have seven computers and have made an office into a computer room, putting in the required electrics, tables, chairs, window and floor covering, so we can now offer the girls hands-on experience, instead of just theory. Again thanks to our friends, the school is now on the Internet, a boon to the staff as well as the students.

7   In the future, we see the school expanding massively. We need to establish an agricultural department of the school, offering gardening skills, land skills, accruing livestock, producing crops etc.; skills to be used at home and allied to business studies.

8   We could and should build workshops to offer not only the academically-orientated girls a career, but the other intelligent and talented girls opportunities to develop: health and beauty, secretarial courses, child care, mechanics, plumbing etc.

9   Sports fields and sports-related courses. The list is ambitious, but let's aim high.

There are things we cannot do. For example, we are introducing a scheme whereby all the teachers are observed teaching. At home, the observation sheet would comment on content, how the teaching time was broken down into different sections, differentiation, resources used, participation and involvement of pupils, pupils on task etc., etc. The students here have one resource: the teacher. Often not even books. The only ones to use photocopies of worksheets are Anne and I, because we can buy our own. So we cannot attempt to impose a different work practice here. The students themselves are not trained or have no experience of participation; their job is to listen and take notes. What we can do, however, is make sure the syllabus is being taught (in the past, malpractice was not an infrequent occurrence), that the work trawls reveal that progress is being made, and, most of all, that the teachers are encouraged.

The Girls

All this reflection without mentioning the principal actors in the drama. What can you say? What can you say of their resilience, their good and refreshing sense of fun and humour, their manners and kindness, their spirituality? They are wonderful. Of course they need the odd reminder. We all do. But what many of them have to endure... There is a vast pool who need counselling, need nurturing, need healing. Many are orphans (one parent lost). Some are full or complete orphans. Many are children of polygamous marriages, unhappily treated or mistreated by stepmothers; all of them are poor. We are here, and by 'we' I mean all the staff, the directors, the VMs. We are here for them, to give them the opportunities they need so desperately and deserve so much.

16.02.2005 Winnie the Winner

If you knew Winnie like I know Winnie; oh, oh, oh, what a girl!
Winnie is one of the school workers. She works on the school compound, sweeping, cleaning, doing all sorts of jobs. She does them with a smile on her face. In fact, her most appealing virtue, character trait, is her sense of humour and sense of fun. Winnie will laugh at anything, especially my attempts to speak a few local phrases. Every day is a gift from God, and she extracts from it, minute by minute, the maximum fun and gaiety she can. It goes without saying that she is a tremendous worker, steady, thorough, seemingly tireless.

Winnie also works for us in the house once a week, and, as well as her wages, she gets a bottle of beer, which is always a case of great rejoicing! There have been occasions when Anne and Winnie have been found playing netball or catchball in the living room. A sense of fun allied to girlish giggles; a capturing of or reversal to childhood.

Winnie has three beautiful children. And it came home to us once again what poverty is: it's not the dramatic face of poverty, but the ordinary, wear-and-grind-you-slowly-down face of poverty. This incident is in no way remarkable here. The children are in junior school and have just returned to school. In the course of morning greetings and pleasantries, Anne asked how they were and how they were getting on. It must be stressed that Winnie did not ask for anything; indeed, she would have said nothing were it not for Anne's inquiry, but it came out that she could not afford the money for school dinners, so, along with many others, they would go without a meal all day. Anne immediately gave Winnie 30,000 shillings (ten pounds), which would feed the three of them for the whole term. Winnie was overcome, hugged Anne, whooped shrills of delight and did a little dance. The gift was unsolicited, unlooked for, unexpected and most welcome.

Winnie, like so many others, does not wear her poverty on her sleeve or on her face. On her face she wears a smile, and in her eyes she wears a twinkle. She lives for the moment. Oh, that we all could.

16.02.2005 Incident on the Thursday after Ash Wednesday

Coming back from the dining hall, which we have rearranged and on which we are trying to impose a modicum of civilisation (before, it represented a scene out of the last days of the Roman Empire!), I come across Sheila in her classroom. Sheila is thirteen or fourteen, but is so slim and slight she could pass for an eleven-year-old, with a round, angelic, fine-featured face.

I ask if she is not well, sitting at her desk with her head in her arms.

No, she is fine.

Why is she not in the dining hall, eating her lunch?

She is fasting.

Why?

So God will forgive her her sins.

Is it because it's Lent?

Yes, sir.

God has already forgiven you your sins, and God loves you with all his heart. Now go and eat your lunch. That's what He wants you to do.

It brings a lump to your throat.

05.03.2005 Marathons

My first outing to a drama festival. The school's first outing to a drama festival, or, indeed, any festival. It was appropriate that it was a drama festival; dramatic it was.

The 'organisers' (in the circumstances, a term fraught with irony) had written a letter on 14 December. God knows when they posted it, but it arrived about 8 February. There was to be a drama festival in which our branch of the Young Christian Students was invited to take part, the drama to be no more than thirty minutes and not to be entertainment. Right, write and produce a play in two weeks. Let's go.

On several occasions, I tried to contact the organisers to find out the programme, but to no avail. Number unobtainable at this time. Finally, I went to the school at which it was being held, only to be greeted like a saviour, a man with knowledge. They were the hosts, and did I know what was expected of them? How many schools were coming? How many students? I informed them I would endeavour to find out.

At last, the day before the event, I got in touch. How many schools involved? I don't know. How many students? I don't know. How many invitations sent out? Thirty. If each play lasts thirty minutes, that will take well over fifteen hours. Do they expect students or anyone else to watch for fifteen hours? Silence. What is the programme? We are getting one and will phone back at noon.

2.30 p.m. I phone. You didn't return my call at noon. I had problems. Programme? We'll give it tomorrow. I then informed the hapless lady that this was by far the most ill-organised event I had ever heard of in my life, and added a few other words of wisdom.

I told the kids we would in no way grace this shambles with our presence. They were heartbroken. I warned them what to expect: waiting around in the hot sun; people not knowing what was going on; being made to wait heaven knows how long before we got on; when we would eat etc. But they were sold on going and performing. Against my better judgement.

It was termed a 'drama festival'. It should have been termed a 'melodrama festival'. It was extraordinary. Our little play was refined, demure. Restrained by comparison. And where they got the term 'not entertainment', God knows. It was explosive! It was burlesque, vaudeville, knockabout, high-blown, no-holds-barred, *Tom and Jerry*, *Popeye*, unrestrained energy and in-your-face direct fun. The energy! The acting! Great! OK, subtlety was not in the equation. When people were informed they had AIDS (the theme of the festival), they didn't grow pale; they fell to the floor, writhed in agony, screamed and had to be dragged off. Every play had such eruptions of emotions. Wailing? Wailing? Jerusalem has heard nothing like it. And when the lads went to have 'jiggy-jig' (known in polite circles as sexual encounters), boy, did they show you with pointing, gyrating and general glee what they were engaged in. It was *Rambo* compared with *The Remains of the Day*. They paint in LARGE PRIMARY COLOURS. Great fun.

The host school was just charming. All the kids wonderful. Our girls were a credit to the school and their parents, and they loved being out and doing their play. The adjudicators were cretins and I don't know what, if any, their credentials are (criticism of all the students harsh – it makes them feel superior), but we did not come anywhere near last (everything is a competition here!). An experience and a revelation.

Wow.

That was Saturday.

On Sunday, I thought I'd have a sleep in. At 7.35 a.m., there is a knock on the door. Four girls have to go to confession at 8 a.m. before receiving Confirmation (why do they always come to us and no one else, like the teacher on duty?). Meet me at the gate in fifteen minutes. Crowe leaps into the shower (a loose term) whilst shaving, gets dressed and is at the gate in fifteen minutes. No girls. Twenty minutes later they arrive and Crowe demonstrates about their tardiness, we are here for their benefit etc., etc. This is Africa. The girls give Crowe a look which is a mixture of incomprehension, pity and bewilderment. We go up to the church where the ceremony will take place at 10 a.m. to find the place already filling up from all the outlying villages.

The Mass, thank God, is to be held outside. We arrive at 10 a.m. discreetly, unobtrusively, near the back. Oh, no. We are ushered to the front; indeed, on the altar, in full view of everyone. A place of honour, but you have to stay awake throughout and feign absolute interest in everything everyone says. There is no quick escape.

In the event, the liturgy was magnificent. Hundreds to be confirmed; all the girls garlanded with natural flowers in their hair, and the boys with one flower. A beautiful sight. And the singing, the dancing! To see the PP gathering the baptismal tickets (certificates), swaying, swinging rhythmically down the aisles; the altar boys dancing and ushering up to the front an old man who really knew how to move, his body in perfect rhythm and going in ten different directions at once. Sheer joy. It was David dancing before the Lord, with exuberance, joy, gladness. It was the Old Testament made real: celebration, praise, laughter (and what greater praise than laughter?).

The exuberance was punctuated by the most interminable speeches imaginable. The Africans make it an art form. I had never really appreciated the full impact of the phrase 'boring the arse off someone'. And it is a myth that the Africans don't mind it. They are just polite, because they are as bored as the rest of us. But oh, everybody speaks.

The bishop, charming, educated, urbane, whipped through the confirmandi in about forty minutes, going for the Guinness Book of Records; but done with a smile, a charm and grace as he went between them row by row. Meanwhile, the choir sang, chanted, danced. Here, they do liturgy with a capital L.

After four hours, I was drooping. And then, at 2 p.m., the bishop gave a farewell speech, which was excellent but lasted for thirty-five minutes. The bishop had just visited the war-torn north, Gulu, and I can testify to everything he said. It was the right message, but the wrong time. He had seen everything I had seen and was very moved by it, but it does beg the question of why it took the hierarchy eighteen years to go there! One of the questions that puzzled us was why the hierarchy did not take a more overt and proactive role in defending the people of the north. Well, at last and at least, they are beginning to do so.

Throughout this long service, the children – little, little two, three, four-year-olds – behaved impeccably. How?

The service ended with the people of the parish giving the bishop gifts: money, fruit, eggs, several hens, two turkeys, a kid and a calf. One wonders how he got them into his vehicle!

We arrived back, jaded; bewildered, if not bewitched (a word you do not use lightly here), but very happy.

What a wonderful weekend. How was yours?

05.03.2005 *Death in the Afternoon, and Evening, and Night and Morning*

I don't think I was fully aware of what culture shock, or, perhaps more accurately, culture clash was. It is disturbing. It plays with and throws into disarray your preconceptions, your certainties; certainties you didn't even know you had: unspoken, taken for granted, the way things are.

Take death, for example. In the West, certainly in Britain, death comes wrapped up in ceremony, procedure. It is not immediate; near, but distanced by silence, remoteness, by the whole mechanism of undertakers and the process of laying out, viewing and laying to rest. Even with all that, we handle death awkwardly, with hesitancy, hedging around, because of our deep sensibility and our anxiety not to cause pain or hurt, or even (a dreaded offence) to intrude. We do not even use the word 'death', but euphemisms like 'passing away', 'going to the other side' or whatever. We find it hard to talk about and find it difficult to know what to say directly to the bereaved. There is enormous sympathy and much feeling, much tender feeling, but its expression is often mute, and we delegate our expression to symbols and silence; flowers, cards and, sometimes, letters. Such is the enormity of death, it paralyses the normal human contact and interaction. It is seen as tragic and final.

In Ireland, in my young days, it was not so. A different culture prevailed: more immediate; more accepting.

The one exception to this code of silence and hushed tone is the magnificent Requiem Mass, my favourite of all masses. It is so full of hope and new beginnings. Apart from the Dies Irae, which is enough to put the screaming heebee jeebies up anyone, the ringing tone of the resurrection, of life, of victory, is sounded throughout. But this runs counter to the rest of the experience: the kind cups of rattling tea; the searching for the right word; the embarrassed silences when the spouse or child walks into the room; the wet, windy, cold gravesides. Thank God nowadays the family and friends can give a small oration at the funeral.

Here, it is altogether different. The horrible ugly phrase is 'life is cheap'. It means death is so frequent, comes in so many guises, that it lacks shock or even surprise. Life is fleeting, not held on to.

Last week, Christopher was drowned. I had met him briefly, when he called on his grandmother at her compound. She has a host of grandchildren and great-grandchildren, and some time ago I wrote about this wonderful lady. She feeds her brood, nurtures them, cossets them, loves them. Christopher was twenty, helped his beloved gran with her cattle. She sold them to pay for the building of her new house, but kept four calves, one of which, on his request, she had promised to him as a dowry. Which doting gran can refuse a grandson?

Christopher had many friends, and some of them were teaching him to fish in the swamps: another string to his bow; another means of eating or, perhaps, of vending. They taught him how to manoeuvre the boat, how to control it and how to cast off a fishing line. Then they let him try himself under their expert eye. Unfortunately, they had neglected to teach him how to swim, or to ascertain whether he could or not. He reached the far shore, alighted from the boat to remove his shirt, and, as he did so, the boat began to slip away. Instinctively, he jumped in after it. The boys, to their consternation, saw him go under, resurface several times whilst shouting for help. They frantically raced towards him, but it was too late.

Here, death is different. That is not to say that grief is mitigated, or less searing, or does not cut as deeply. But it seems abrupt, sharp, quickly finished. Christopher's mother was almost suicidal, heartbroken, but the burial and the rites are brief beyond belief. No sooner is there death than there is the burial. The funeral is the next day (the heat), and everyone is buried in their ancestral home; even those who die in the city are transported home to their compound. The pain may be long and enduring, but the committing to earth is swift.

It is above all the frequency of death that robs it of surprise, that gives it that air of being ordinary, a happening of every day from which there is no escape. It fails to register the same shock and outrage that this interruption causes us. In the short time I have been here, there have been funerals every week; malaria, TB, AIDS, commonly road accidents. In the last two days, two young women, both in their early thirties, both with two young children, the youngest five months old, have died. One because the husband refused to give the doctors a bribe and so they neglected her and she died from pneumonia she developed from malaria, and the other from some other disease. And, last night, a child and several adults died in a road accident outside the school. When I commiserated with the cousin of one of the young women, he looked at me and without being at all cynical, said, 'These things happen.'

It is disturbing. Life seems more transitory, more fleeting, precarious and, oddly, more precious. Paradoxically, it heightens the importance of every minute of every day, whilst at the same time reducing it to almost insignificance. Things need to be done and need to be done NOW. But, if they are not, they will be done at another time by someone else. Or not. It is a strange sort of freedom.

09.04.2005 Two Scenes from the Bush

A beautiful, beautiful evening. We drove along a single track to the clearing: six or seven conical-shaped thatched huts in a circle; one for cooking, one for the mother and daughter, and the rest sleeping quarters for the four young men (each his own).

We looked out on endless African fields meeting an endless African sky; green fields growing cassava, sweet potatoes, rice, onions, sorghum, simsim, dodo (greens) and, of course, mangoes. Chairs were arranged outside for the guests. We sat and chatted with the four young men, but not their mother, who is the school cook and was working. Then they proudly showed us around.

They showed me the well, a little further along the fields, where all the local people collected their water. Forget the picturesque little well with the circular stone or brick wall, a bucket and rope. This was an open ditch with water; it is hard to describe, except with the Yeats line: 'mouse-grey waters' and mud. They explained that, after the rainy season, the community would get together and 'clean' it: weed it, shore up the bank, put fresh stones on the side etc. It certainly needed it. They used the water for washing, cooking and even sometimes for drinking (if you leave it long enough in a jar). Drinking water is mainly fetched from a bore hole one and a half kilometres away. Their sister fetched it; it is women's work. After I upbraided them for this, they just laughed, as she did. A lovely, intensely shy young lady.

The four young men. How to describe them? Charming, personable, with warm, open faces, bright eyes and teeth that would make Tom Cruise cringe with envy. And smart! It is a constant source of bafflement and wonder to me how Africans are so smart and so well turned out, with bright, clean, ironed shirts (or dresses etc.), trousers neat, and the whole impression of a positive go-ahead attitude.

I was there (or so I thought) as a guest, because Anne and I are sponsoring one of the boys through his A level. He had called and asked us to come to his home. Well, all right; I had better things to do with my time, but you have to be gracious, exchange a few words – awkward words probably – exchange smiles, which would be genuine, and confirm, if not friendship, at least friendliness and good fellowship.

Then the elder brother took me aside. He had called to see me at school, but I had been busy. He wanted to explain the situation. You see, they had lived there all their lives, but their grandmother, at the behest and persuasion of their aunt, had sold the huts' land and smallholding, and they had to vacate the premises by June. They had a spot to build a house in the adjacent plot, and they had made the bricks (I saw them, 2,000 of them), but they needed the money to build the house. That was why we were there.

We are sponsoring so many people and projects that our 'well' is running dry. I said I couldn't promise anything, I'd have to know the cost and maybe give something towards it etc.

Yes, in one way we were hijacked, hoodwinked, but this is poverty in reality. Where would they go if they didn't come to us? And they are four lively, likely young men, with a lovely sister.

The story of the grandmother and aunt – well, that could make a novel!

Oh, we left with a traditional African gift as honoured guests: a turkey and chicken, alive!

Hope

I met Washington, our bursar, in the waiting room of the doctor's. Precious (a wonderful name), the head's little one, was being treated for malaria. When she got the injection, I think they could hear her in Kenya.

Washington was there with his son because he thought he had typhoid. The test results, however, showed it was malaria, which had been poorly treated (no drugs). I offered to give them a lift back.

By heavens, what a journey! Road? What road? For miles we went over dirt tracks and negotiated potholes as big as Old Trafford before arriving at his house. A lovely house, with a smaller house next door, surrounded by breathtaking scenery, but in the back of beyond and then a little bit further. Immediately, chairs came out for the honoured guests. I apologised, thanked them profusely, but said I had to get back to work; but not before shaking hands with a host of smiling, giggling excited children and demure, polite older ones. Washington's wife, bathed in smiles, was warmth and hospitality itself.

Later that day, I asked Washington to whom all the children belonged. Well, he explained, he had six children, but in 1997, his brother, who had lived next door, had died, as had his two wives, so he took over his brother's six children. Twelve children. I was stunned. I opined that his wife was very generous to do such a thing. His face lit up. 'Oh, yes, she is very kind. Very kind. She took the children in straight away. Yes. Very kind.' You could smell his pride in her. I suggested it must be hard feeding them all, and schooling. Yes, he replied quietly, very hard.

Not once did Washington ask for, look for a shilling. He did not even hint.

A great man. A great wife. A great family.

09.04.2005 *Love Story*

It is a love story: as simple as that. A love story.

I am now the owner of a second or third or fifth-hand car – a Toyota Carib – all the way from Dubai, which cost about 3,000 pounds, or I suppose, 5,000 euros(?). It arrived in the school about 3.30 p.m., delivered by hand by Yussif. And what an arrival!

Immediately, the school truck driver, Philemon, took the keys, drove it outside the house and washed it, to universal approval and acclamation. Everyone followed the car and everyone, including the cleaner, Winnie, proceeded to get in, test the seats, handle the steering wheel, feel the roof, let out whoops and shouts, and generally exhibit great glee and rejoicing. My hand was warmly shaken with great pride and I was warmly congratulated as though I had just become a father. There was the same wonder and excitement about the whole episode.

But this is a love story. It is Philemon's love story, and he displays the same forlorn lovesick look every young man has when he beholds the object of his desire, affection and feverish fantasy. He came and stated that the engine MUST be cleaned, steam cleaned, I imagine, and was gone for three hours, returning to show me its wonderful condition. On Tuesday, he took the car out to make sure the tyre pressures were correct. On the same day, he tested and checked the oil and water. On Wednesday, he checked the oil and water (we hadn't used the car in between) and informed me a small dent was on the outside of the driver's side and must be fixed. It would need repainting, that bit. He then borrowed the car to pick up his O level results (he is a married man with children who did his O level last year – good for him) and went swanning off in it to pick up his certificate and incredibly impress all and sundry who would be at the school.

On the first day we got the car, he said I must go to Kampala, he would drive and when were we going? Yesterday, I drove out with the head to visit a teacher in hospital – hope to God he doesn't find out!

But you know love when you see it. The sudden breathlessness; the gleam in the eye; the lack of concentration; the inappropriate replies to questions; the restlessness until you are with the one who has taken over your life and heart and mind and body and sense and feelings and power of speech; the only compensation for not being with her is to at least talk about her. Yep: it's love. Poor bugger.

Clucking hens and chicks – no – moonstruck, helpless, hopeless love, love, love; that's what it is. Who am I to stand in the way?

19.04.2005 *Light and Dark*

Let it first be said that P. is a lovely girl: tall, slim, very good-looking and eighteen years old. More than that, she is 'laid back', with a lovely sense of humour. We share a running joke, which always ends up with my giving her a 'high five'. When she passes, she sometimes doesn't even look at me; this hand will just shoot out. A great girl.

She has evinced and shown an interest in becoming a nun, which a few of the girls do. She is religious and is part of the 'rosary' group, but not overly so. Just a nice, nice girl.

Which is why I was so taken aback to find that she is the one susceptible to being possessed.

It is not the first time she has had this dreadful experience. Before Mass started, she almost fainted and was carried to the side of the field. Thank God, it was an open air Mass. I thought it was our old friend malaria and rushed back to the house in order to get the car. When I returned, they had transferred her to the sacristy, and then the extraordinary scenes unfolded. There were three of her friends, another man and Fr D. holding her down, or trying to. I moved behind her to stop her banging her head on the concrete floor – God knows what damage she would have done to herself. The wrestling match between her and the rest of us reached some pretty fierce moments. She exhibited immense strength, and sometimes we were unable to hold her down and she would struggle up but not free, and then would kick and bite and try to scratch. During this time she spoke in English and Swahili, but unlike last time, I am told, not in her Kenyan tribe's old language, which she does not know!

Fr D. is wise and experienced in these matters. Throughout, he was anointing her and blessing her with holy water and praying and talking to her, as were her friends. One kept saying, 'Who are you?', but, except for some guttural noises, it elicited no response. She would, in English, sometimes say, 'Why? Why?'

and 'Leave me alone. Leave me alone.' What she said in Swahili, I do not know.

I do know it was an incredible struggle, and afterwards I was covered in sweat and tired. The most amazing thing – well, the second most amazing thing – to discover is how immediate the spirit world is. It is not a little room locked in the dark recesses of your mind with a notice saying 'do not enter'; it is not some remote, distant, far-away place, another world, but it is in this world, here and now: tangible; audible; close, very close. Close encounters of a frighteningly immediate kind!

They administered a sedative after this half-hour or so, and several of us took her to the local clinic (clinic! I'll tell you about that some day), where they kept her for a few hours.

The most amazing thing, however, was not that encounter but a purely human encounter; an encounter with kindness. She was put in the sick bay, one of the small teachers' houses used for the purpose, and her two friends, E. and L., stayed with her, spent the night in the sick bay. I brought them over some fruit and water, for which they thanked me profusely. I thanked them. Oh, these girls. All the attributes you could wish on the world; kindness itself; caring, unfussy, laughing, open, and very concerned for and worried about their friend. That is love; that is unconscious selflessness. I love 'em.

I went to see them first thing in the morning to ask how they and P. had got on. They brightly said, 'Wonderful.' When she woke up, she wanted to go to church. She then relapsed into a sort of sleep, unconsciousness. It must be incredibly exhausting to be possessed. For P. is a good, lovely girl, and, although she suffers this dreadful intrusion, it is unasked for and unwelcome, and its evil does not besmirch or sully her.

Another memorable Sunday.

19.04.2005 *This Letter Was Written…*

This letter was written by my Eng. Lit group. You can tell why I LOVE them just from the letter. I said, 'Oh, I'm going back home next week. What do you think I should tell the people back home?' Here is what they said.

> On behalf of the whole school of St Clare family, the Senior Six literature class would like to salute you all in Jesus' name. It has been a pleasure to have two of your people, that is Mr and Mrs Patrick Crowe, here in St Clare's and Uganda as a whole. They have made an impact in our education, in building up our talents and also in our Christian lives. Through them we also acknowledge your generosity in sending us money to buy more computers, to repair our buildings and to also improve our dining hall to make it a place worth eating from. Your kindness is very much appreciated. St Clare's is a society of girl students who have the desire to excel in their academics and make Uganda a better place to be in the future. We do lack some facilities that could make our dreams and aspirations come true; for example:
>
> 1 We have a library, yes, but it is not well equipped. We lack novels, textbooks for different subjects, plays for literature, and all because we have limited capital to purchase them.
>
> 2 Our laboratory, despite being only one, lacks facilities and equipment required for various sciences; that is, Chemistry, Biology and Physics, and this makes practicals difficult. It also limits the number of students offered sciences in A level, yet many would love to be offered sciences.
>
> 3 We also lack different games and their facilities, like rackets for badminton, bats and tables for table tennis, hockey sticks for hockey, and even though we have a b/ball court it's not cemented and is therefore inefficient, and because of this students don't engage in different games to find out where their talents lie.

4   Despite all these physical lacks, we have students here in school who are brilliant in class but, because their parents are poor, they lack fees and end up dropping out of school. Some of them pass highly their O level, but lack of fees or sponsorship make them drop out of school to be home, thus limiting their chances to be prominent figures in society.

These are some of the things we lack in St Clare's that lag us from succeeding, but through your generous giving we believe we shall get them and we will work hard to make Uganda and the whole world in general a better place. Thanks a million for your charity and we pray that the good God may bless you abundantly.

Sincerely

Aujo Christine

Makale Peris

Mukhwana Anette

Jepchumba Janete

Santa Nambozo

Kemunto Clare

I did not influence their writing in any way. These are their words, although they may have picked up the phrase 'thanks a million' from me. But that is all.

It says it all.

04.06.2005 *Truth and Appearance*

We are back in school and it is all hands to the pump. It's great, but there is so much to do, thank God. We are busy writing out forms and ordering books (wow, we could spend all the money on books. One subject teacher had until now one textbook; now he'll have way over a hundred!). Our main problem is getting the latrines emptied! The girls are excited about all the books, about the sports equipment, about the new furniture, and, it must be confessed, so am I.

But truth and appearance.

I love our school, and I love the girls. But even they are cocooned. I look out the window; today we have a public holiday – the Ugandan martyrs – and the sun is, of course, shining: perhaps that's part of the problem, because, paradoxically, it conceals rather than reveals; it lulls one into a false sense of well-being.

Two papers or reports I have just read paint the true picture. You may or may not be interested, but I have to tell the story. When you read this, picture not a people, at least the immediate people, going round with grim faces, but a people ever ready to smile and endure; but for how long?

The first report is an account, in both senses of the word, of our district, Pallisa, in which Budaka resides. It is described as poverty-stricken (and that word 'stricken' is well worth dwelling on; it is like a man or woman being constantly struck, repeatedly struck), peopled by a heterogeneous community. The people's daily income is below one US dollar. Every time you go out, you see people working and frantically looking for work, for a few coppers. The chairman of the district calls for love, tolerance and teamwork.

I have mentioned often girls' place in society. Supported by UNICEF, they now have child-friendly schools. Sounds good, doesn't it, until you realise that, as girls drop out of education at primary level owing to pregnancy brought on by rape or defilement, they have set up a system of counselling to encourage them back into school. The report gives one(!) example of success last year.

There then follows a wishlist of all that the chair would like to see: improvement in infrastructure; more access to electricity for rural people (less than 10% of the population has it); diversification of crops, since 99% of Pallisa is agriculture: afforestation and citrus fruit production etc., etc. All this is splendid, but when you consider that only 39% of the water in the area is considered safe, that the one good hospital is old and decaying and, despite an increase of drugs, disease is far outstripping the supply, one begins to get the scale of the problems. There is now what is known as 'universal primary education'. The primary school population has risen from 55,255 children to 171,000 in recent times. It is great to say everyone can be freely educated, but, if a child ends up in a class of 150 or even 200, what's the point, especially if you don't feed them?

But I end this part with the plea from this poor beleaguered chairman. God knows, as with many politicians here, one wonders what part he plays. But his plea seems heartfelt.

> We must not forget the peaceful co-existence of the diverse ethnic groupings of Pallisa has been concretised by intermarriage and migratory practices over decades. It would be naïve for anyone to tamper with this tranquillity, and we should be mindful not to start a genocide our children will innocently live to bitterly experience when we are not there to reverse or harmonise the explosive situation... Rwanda, Darfur, Palestine.

Fine words and true; yet the bad governance of this poor country has made the situation explosive.

The next report comes from the grandly-titled 'Civil Society Organisations for Peace in Northern Uganda': a group of NGOs and other groups working in the north and pooling their resources and carrying out detailed analysis of what is taking place. It makes for sorry reading, and holds the government and the international community to account.

The difficulty is in the use of the word 'Uganda'. There is no such place. It is a geographically-defined region, with a host of tribes and fifty-six languages, each tribe holding allegiance to itself and none to 'Uganda'.

The people in the north, especially the Acholi people, have been thrown to the dogs and savages by the government.

The paper is entitled 'Humanitarian Protection Threats in Northern Uganda'. It reports that it is the world's most serious protection crisis; the civilian population is the principal strategic target and victim of violence; there is gross abuse of international law by the government troops and rebels; the rebels (Lord's Resistance Army) inflict a cocktail of psychological and physical violence, and the government has failed in its duty of protection.

The process of forced displacement is horrendous. It is accompanied by violence, looting and rape, and this by the so-called protectors. This displacement destroys livelihoods, severs civilian life with the land, creates life-threatening living conditions with an acute shortage of food and water. There are the usual suspects of rape, defilement and STDs.

All this from the government forces.

There is a slow, if any, transition from ancestry-based identity to a national identity. The report pleads for international intervention, and government beneficial control and interest. It has been going on for nineteen years. It recommends a national language and a structured, careful documentation of the history of Uganda taught in all schools.

This is just the merest outline. But c'mon, tell your MPs and anyone in the media or wherever, your bishops, whoever. Tell them this people's plight.

The most important meeting of the last sixty years takes place in Gleneagles when the G8 meet. Pray that it succeeds. I've written to Gordon Brown and my girls are writing this week. Do likewise.

What is poverty to our girls? These are the lucky ones, but I quote from a letter one of our girls wrote to her sponsor, a friend of mine:

> I will never stop thanking you madam because I did not have any alternative. I knew my learning could end soon. I didn't complete last term's fees and this term's were also needed. It was difficult

for my mother to pay for all of us (three boys, four girls). So she told me to just go to school and plead with them to allow me to stay until she got the money. Even now she has ulcers because of stress. All of us depend on her and she has no well paid job. I left her at home when she was looking for money to go for treatment.

When I returned to school, I received the miraculous message from Mr and Mrs Crowe that they had got for me you to help me lift me up.

07.06.2005 Hi: a Letter Written by Kerunto

Hi,

Am an African lady and, I believe, the generation of tomorrow. First of all I want to thank both of you for your movement, 'Make Poverty History'. Your efforts to eradicate poverty in Africa are the greatest aid Africa could ever receive from you. It means a lot to us that some people out there care for us. Africa is a rich country; the use of what we have and the appreciation in what we possess is what we lack, but I believe if we are sensitised about them we will no longer be deprived of our humanity because of poverty. Every day I wake and when I look around I see suffering, I see the tears of hungry children, I see illiteracy, I see the endless corpses lying around because of wars, I see people flee homes because of lack of security. Every day I hear a child is thrown away. Why? Because one cannot afford what he/she needs and the mother herself is too malnourished to even have a drop of milk for the baby. I walk around and see endless street children, out in the cold, bellies too big to be covered by the tattered clothes, hunger their best company, begging the order of the day, children carrying children and my heart's wounds grow fresh, the pain becomes so unbearable that the tears can't be held back. The poverty cycle is too hard to break as people live below the poverty line. Poverty is chewing up Africa at a high rate and with every bite, Africa faces death row. You know today you get something close to a meal; tomorrow, or for another couple of weeks, your luck isn't promised. Children, mothers stay naked; in coldness they get fever and death follows. Medical care is so far from what they call home that before one gets there a soul is lost. A soul that could be tomorrow's future. You look into a child's eyes and suffering is seen, hunger is felt and a child deprived of his future because of poverty is spelled out. Every morning a child wakes up with hope for a bright day, but every night he goes to bed with 'hopes' shattered. Corruption slowly crops up. The rich become self-centred. All they want is the best for themselves and their

The school compound

Children arriving at school

Local ladies

Me with Michael, the IT teacher

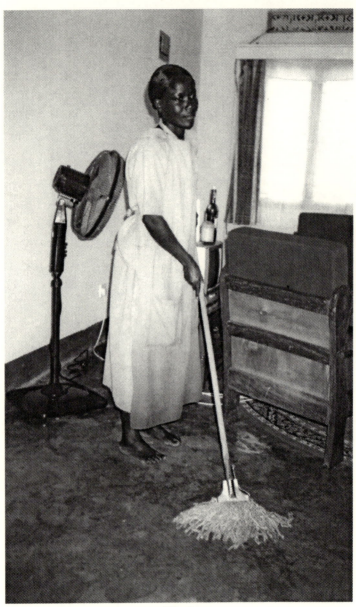

Winnie

Teacher Christopher on a field trip

Drama group '05 rehearsing for the drama festival. I wrote a play called AIDS. AIDS was the title given by the YCS, who ran the festival.

St Clare's day

The school driver – Philemon.
We kept a supply of sodas as 'thank-yous' for jobs done.

Maureen Mugodo with 'Cat' (left) and Jessie (right), the girls who worked in the Leonard Cheshire home.

Sister Cosmas

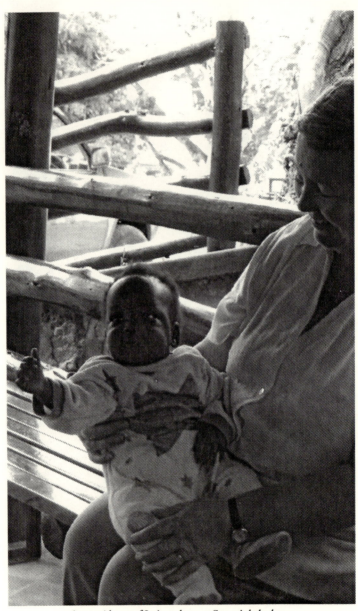

Anne with one of Joe's orphans at Sanyu's baby home.

Me with Lucy

The teachers with 'Paddy'.

The computer room is useable at last.

families. To get a job, one is forced to bribe or 'know somebody', so no money, no job. Unemployment is also poverty, as one has no money, and due to this one might prostitute herself, and diseases are spread where millions of worthy lives are lost. Lack of money means the public funds are embezzled. Sent aid is pocketed by the top officials, leaving the rest suffering, all because of poverty. Investors themselves never think of building up the place they have invested in; instead, they manipulate the labourers and in the end repatriate the profits back into their own countries, leaving poverty and suffering behind. Debts are so great that even Africa herself finds them difficult to carry. Paying all these debts leaves her next to death because as she pays them she keeps being poor. On top of it all, unfair trade terms are practised on her. Because of poverty, agriculture is the only way out, but still her agricultural goods aren't considered. Why? Because she has low technology and she lacks cash to improve it, which is poverty. Protectionism is also practised, where Africa is not allowed to trade some of her goods because 'others' want their goods to dominate, and I am left to wonder: is it because it is a black continent or because other countries just want the best for themselves? Sir Brown and Hon. Blair, mother Africa sobs, her tears are endless, she cries for the souls she is losing, she sobs for the debts she has to pay but doesn't have the means to, she wants to support herself but keeps falling down with each step. If the unfair trade terms are done away with, if the debts are just excused and if people are sensitised to do their best and stop corruption, Africa will stand and no more corpses will be seen, no people will sleep hungry, streets will be rid of begging children and suffering will no longer be spelled out. Sir Brown and Hon. Blair, Africa needs you. Look upon her with eyes of mercy and, for the love of God, help her. You two and any supporting the movement have hearts of angels, and you have all our support. Our prayers are also with you and, even if you don't succeed, which I suppose will be the case, your efforts will with so much joy and thanks be appreciated. May the Good Lord bless the work of your hands, and all the best in 'Making Poverty History'.

Compiled by Kerunto

25.06.2005 Forgotten War (Discarded People)

Most of the time, I am not aware of it; I'm involved totally, blinkered, locked into the minutia of daily life: has that bill been paid? Has the week's food been ordered? Why have we run out of tube lighting again? Where did I put...? etc., etc. The little 'arrows' that assail us every working day of our lives. Now and again, however, another perspective breaks through and you catch a glimpse of the bigger picture and you freeze.

Fr Carlos Rodriquez
I met him briefly in Gulu, in a workshop to do with deeply traumatised children. Or, perhaps better, we shared for a short time the same space and time.

Fr Carlos is not charismatic. In a crowded room, you wouldn't notice him. In an empty room, it would require an effort. He is reticent to the point of anonymity, an absence rather than a presence. This is in no way to judge or condemn him. Perhaps that day he was preoccupied. He has a great deal to occupy him.

Yet this almost absurdly quiet man is a thorn in the side of the government and the army. He does a lot of work with the Peace and Justice group in Gulu in the north. These are the people who live in the beautiful and lush and fertile land, some of the richest in Uganda. But they have been driven from their homes by the army, forced to live in camps (one step up from concentration camps), and they're left to sink into despair, ill health and apathy. A once-proud people, now beaten, neglected, fed by the World Food Programme.

Those around the villages who have not been driven from their land silently 'commute': walk into Gulu every night to find protection in the corridors of hospitals, doorways, churches, streets, from infants with three-year-olds upwards, without blankets, without food and often without parents. This has been going on for eighteen years.

This slow strangulation of a people, this quiet persistent tsunami, suits the government's agenda. The UN regards it as the worst humanitarian crisis today.

But Fr Carlos does not neglect or discard the people. He visits. He visits to show solidarity, to listen, to heal, to be one with. It does not suit the Powers That Be that he should draw attention to these people or their plight. So they harass, bully, threaten to lock him up or chase him away. They have no intention of opening the camps or letting the eyes of the world rest on them. This silent, quiet, courageous man, who draws attention not to himself but to the persecuted, is a threat.

But who is to listen? How much suffering does it take for the international community to holler 'ENOUGH!'? How many young girls must be raped; how many boys and girls be forced to maim, murder and torture their own parents or relatives and live – no, not live, but exist – in abject fear and terror, before we call a halt to this obscene madness? How many thousands must be robbed; violently, sadistically robbed of their childhood? God must weep. Countless mothers do.

Pray for Fr Carlos. Pray for the people. Do more than that. Write. Write to the politicians of your own countries. Write to the churchmen, to the newspapers, to the TV, to the radio. Shout out, and bring this sorry atrocity to a close.

05.07.2005 *Country of Contrasts*

I suppose, like all people, each country is a hotchpotch of contradictions and contrasts. Yesterday, a wonderful experience of what Yeats called 'moments of glad grace'. In the local marketplace, sitting in my car, having just brought a girl to the health centre, watching several small children play. Two three-year-old boys practising the astonishing skill all Africans have, balancing pieces of paper on their head. Walking and then tipping the paper from their heads deliberately, as though unloading sacks of coal or whatever. Then they spot me, and, gleefully, they all run over to stare delightedly at the *msungu* – white man – and shake my hand and run away laughing. Beautiful.

And then David, a local taxi driver who drives us to Kampala when we go (I would never drive to Kampala myself; I like living), says, quite matter-of-factly, 'Of course, some Africans are mad. They will rob you of 10,000 shillings (four pounds or six euros) and then kill you so that you cannot identify them.' David is a well-built, stocky lad of twenty-seven. He grins. He grins when he talks and probably when he sleeps. Jovial, jolly. A very good driver, alert, smart, cautious, never taking a risk. Always ready to please. He shows me the top of his head, which bears a large scar running almost over the entire skull. When he was eighteen, some men hired his taxi, robbed it and left him for dead, having struck him with a sort of hammer with a sharpened edge. For some reason, David survived. He grins and says, yes, some Africans are mad.

And then there is the nobly-named Hilary – such wonderful old-fashioned names! – who is an entomologist who works for the government. He was ill a couple of years ago and had to pay a massive amount for his kidney operation. In fact, the whole family had to club together to pay for it. Since then, he has had a motorbike accident, which shook him up considerably. Hilary is at retiring age. He is tired, exhausted. But Hilary cannot retire, like thousands and thousands of others, because the government will not pay their pensions. They will not pay it for years, if they pay it at all, and most die before they receive their pensions. Yet there is no revolution!

And crime. Astonishing. The police here manage to combine the qualities of corruption and ineptness to an exemplary degree. So you can see all your dearly-held liberal values being sucked out the window. The law is taken into your own hands, and summary justice dealt swiftly and ruthlessly. Mbale, our local town, has a reputation throughout Uganda as being rough, tough. There is a sort of vigilante group whose relationship with the law and police has yet to be established, which, for some strange reason, goes under the name of 'the Wembley Mob', and it visits revenge on various unsavoury characters. There was a gang of seven thugs in Mbale who were threatening and intimidating the local people. Someone told the Wembley Mob. They descended, raided. Found grenades, guns, knives etc. They paraded the seven members and asked the locals what they wanted to do. They shot the seven members of the gang dead on the spot. End of robberies. Now, if a thief is caught, he is either burned to death, clubbed to death or knifed to death. Where I would say 'WHAT?', they say, ' And…?'. With raised eyebrows. 'So…?'

I am sure, if I looked at the stuff that goes on back home, I'd see the same contrasts. It just catches me unawares, that's all.

10.07.2005 Latrines, Loos and Laptops

OK, OK, OK. They're not laptops, but it sounded better than 'freestanding table computers'. But you get the idea. The highs and the lows (if you'll pardon the pun) of running a school.

The lows – the loos, or the latrines. There seems to be a common African failing of – or better, non-recognition of the importance of – maintenance. The latrines have not been emptied for years, and, indeed, for over two years one set has been unused, cutting the number of latrines available in half. The bold Crowe, of course, says enough is enough! Oh, yes? Do you know, have you any idea, how hard it is to get loos emptied? Being a fool, I thought I would ask the National Water and Sewerage Corporation to either do it or advise me where I could get it done. Eejit. To letters there were answers none. To a visit in person there was a shrug of the shoulders and the information that they do not do it now! At last, by dint of inquiry amongst hospitals etc., we have found someone, but he wants to charge 50% more because there is a *msungu* (white man) involved. Ah! But they also want a pit dug first.

Do not appeal to health and safety, or the fact we have 300 young ladies boarding, or hygiene. Just find a private company and negotiate.

So, while your minds are fixed on the nobility of the calling, I'm dealing in... well... shit shovelling!

And the kitchens. We have three big missionary-type pots in which all cooking is done, two of which have not worked for three years and the last of which has lost its chimney. It's a wonder the cooks have not died of asphyxiation.

And the transfer of funds. We have the money; it's waiting; I've already spent it, but getting the directors to actually keep an appointment so we can open the account... well, there you go.

But the good, no, the great news:

We are changing our computer room to a large classroom,

have upgraded them, bought a new server(?), another machine, things that protect the computers when there is a power cut etc., got two teachers enrolled to do maintenance courses and networking, and, lads, the excitement. And all on the Internet! Oh, happy days. Kids gambolling on the highways.

So the money we raised is going to all sorts of enterprises: mainly to books, but also computers, latrines, sport equipment, musical instruments, and, importantly, very importantly, mosquito nets. We, or you, have bought every child in the school a net, which should massively reduce the rate of infection. Let me share with you a letter handed in which gives an inkling of the kids' response. Usually, letters handed in are begging, but this said:

Dear Sir,

I write this letter to say thanks for the nets you bought for us. Some of us, that is one thing we could never dream of using ourselves. I thank you sir for making me know the meaning of life by getting for me what I could not afford.

May God shower you with blessings and grant you a long life. Otherwise I thank you sir very much though I don't have anything to pay you in return to your kindness. Thank you, sir.

Appreciates

Wasike Jeanette

The nets, by the way, cost two pounds each!

So I'm off to get someone to locate a spot in which to dig my pit and measure the diameter of the chimneys, then find someone to put them in. And organise the scraping and cleaning of the kitchen, whitewash it and buy the paint so all the school can have a brush-up. Oh, and mark the books and prepare my A level classes. Isn't life fun?

We have an ambition to offer the kids vocational courses.

10.07.2005 Was It Needless Death After All?

'If you have tears, prepare to shed them now.'

It is said that a million deaths are a statistic; one death a tragedy. My mind has been much on death these last few days. I have felt very close to home, and very distant. The elation of winning the elections, heightened by the fact I did not think we would win it, and so the sheer joy. The good it will do the Londoners, especially the neglected East End. And then the tragedy of the terrorist attacks. I was informed that night that my son, in London on business, missed it by twenty minutes. He was walking to Liverpool Street from King's Cross. That just made it even more immediate.

Once more, in spite of the reprehensible and savage attack, goodness shone through. But your mind immediately goes to the people of Iraq who suffer this daily.

This morning, Fr David, who embodies dignity and wisdom, a loving, kind old priest, prayed for the people of England, bombed, he said, 'by those who do not care', and he prayed that, if any were called unprepared, the Good Lord would remember the goodness in their heart and the good they always intended to do. It was very touching, because it was heartfelt.

But we also prayed for Daniel.

This is poverty in action. Daniel was three months old. His father, one of the staff, came to me to say he was ill, vomiting, high temperature etc. The usual suspect, malaria, was the probable cause. Of course he had to miss class, not to worry at all, and I gave him a few quid for the drugs (you have to pay for everything).

You learn every day. When the little one got ill, the reaction around the compound was as if it were expected. Both twins rarely survive, because 'bringing up two is very difficult, and one will thrive, and usually one will wither. Not intentionally, but that is what happens.' To say I was flabbergasted by this attitude is putting it mildly.

But Daniel. In the West there would be an outcry. They took him into the private hospital – 'private' in the sense that you pay, 'hospital' in the sense that it comprises a couple of shabby offices, a thing called a ward, an absent doctor and a nurse and two so-called administers of drugs.

Daniel developed bronchitis. They got his temperature down. Later on, it rose, and rose. The nurse became anxious and asked for the drugs to lower it – repeatedly. She asked again and again, but she was forgotten or ignored, and lethargy won the day. Eventually, the parents, who have that African patience, could wait no more and decided to move him to Kampala, a three-and-a-half-hour drive and, to them, an enormous expense, even if by public transport. They did arrive at St Francis's hospital, but too late. Daniel's little excursion into life was over.

At the funeral, the day after, Daniel's father wept. And then he apologised for not marking his exam papers yet, but they would be done.

Doesn't shock make us react in the strangest ways?

Daniel's father wept. So did the world.

04.08.2005 *Vignettes of Africa*

'YOU SIT THERE.'

He was the second or third or whatever outer, outer secretary in the outer office.

I replied, not in a whisper, 'Is that an order or an invitation?'

For a moment I saw the assuredness, confidence go out of his eye, not helped by the muffled laughter of one of his colleagues. For such polite, friendly people, they can be very abrupt.

Like all doctors' surgeries and offices, there is a hushed silence, broken only by embarrassed whispers from those visiting. I continued to talk to my companions in a normal voice, but it sounded very loud in those circumstances. Blow 'em! Aren't we sometimes so childish?

We had asked for a visit. Indeed, we had previously travelled down to ask for a visit. This was a well-established vocational school, a darling of the government, government sponsored and a great success. A large school, in number and acreage. It has 1,300 children and does all sorts of vocational courses. It also draws its pupils from the upper set.

We had asked when we should come. We were told that, when we came, we would see the two heads of department immediately.

We arrived at 9.45 a.m. But this is Africa. One head of department didn't show up, and the other kept us waiting for an hour and a half.

We waited in the staff room for a good while. We were ushered in. A large staff room, as there are fifty teachers. Desks all round the room; substantial desks. About a dozen teachers, leisurely marking books and idly chatting; the odd banter and exchange of words. Relaxed. This was – is – a successful school and had the confident air of such. The teachers were most welcoming in their hellos and smiles, and some, on entering, warmly shook our hands. Good.

In the middle of the room, four settees; two facing two. Civilised. As the teacher seated on one of the settees, on the end, chatted to his colleagues whilst reading some document from a large folder – an older, genial man, with laughing eyes and an utterly at ease posture – to my amazement, I suddenly saw there were two girls of about fourteen or fifteen lying prostrate on the floor, faces down.

'This one is in trouble, not for the first time. Bullying a senior one girl.'

'Not much of a bull for bullying.'

General laughter.

Back to the folder.

'Mmm. Says here she was very good at drama… and sport. Don't know where she learnt bullying.'

Reads. Opens up other folder.

'Ah, yes. Mnn. Well you two, we don't want to see you again.'

Then, without malice or any sort of viciousness, grabs a cane from the floor and wallop, wallop, wallop. Not vicious, but smarting.

The girls get up and, crying, I think more from humiliation than pain, leave the room. As they leave, a teacher shouts:

'And when I see your mother, Maureen, I'll tell her.'

Later, the teacher, on his way out, says to me in a very friendly way, 'Got to mould these girls.'

Wow.

Lovely teachers. Not much help, though.

Mass at Mbale

Went to Mass at Mbale instead of the usual parish church, as we were staying over there.

It is a good-sized church with all the characteristics of a TARDIS. No matter how many people are in a bench, a full bench, they still manage to shoo in some more!

Indeed, a full church. But the extraordinary thing, for our eyes from the jaded West, is the astonishing number of young men in the congregation, and all join in the singing. All are smartly dressed, and, as for the choir and Sunday best, look at this for being dressed to the nines.

The next thing is the wondrous sound. Whilst the organ warms up to take a run at the next hymn, it wheezes and sneezes, and for all the world you can (I promise this is true) you can hear fiddles tuning up, so you think you're about to join in an American barn dance. Then at last the box gets into gear and the choir starts singing – beautifully. Mostly they sing in one of the local languages, and at each part of the Mass they sing, and sing, and sing. For example, the bidding prayers last for ages because after each prayer they sing an invocation for some time. And so with each part; the Our Father is beautiful and very long, lasting longer than the Sermon on the Mount. Yet suddenly, in between the readings, they will softly sing 'Then sings my soul, my Saviour God to Thee'. Wonderful.

Ah, but the priest. What can I say about the priest? He cajoles, lectures, part comedian, part magistrate, charismatic, held in awe and fear and love; well, that's my impression. It is not just a sermon, but entertainment, and he speaks beautiful English. However, my threshold of boredom is very low and after forty-five minutes my brain is numb, as, indeed, is my bum. Having heard and sometimes even listened to five million, four hundred and forty-four thousand sermons, I can see where they are going, and, fascinating though it was, he could have said it in six minutes. I did not seem to participate so much as to observe. My fault, I'm sure, but difficult.

As for the priest in our parish (which is huge; the church is huge; the congregation huge): a lovely man, but he could bore for Africa. We don't have as many young men because his Masses last up to and beyond three hours! It is a myth that Africans like it; they all complain, but no one dare approach!

Everyone should witness these occasions. Religion is so strong over here; not just Catholics, but every persuasion and hue and colour of Christianity and Islam. Everyone.

04.08.2005 The Birthday Party

Forget Harold Pinter; it was more C S Lewis. The most amazing party I have ever been to.

Two girls approached me. They wanted to have a party for their friend Stella in the dorm after prep (study) from 9 p.m. till 10 p.m. (or even after!). She was nineteen.

I thought of nineteen-year-olds' birthday parties at home, and young girls getting as legless as they could in as short a time as possible.

OK. And yes, they could borrow my CD player, and thank you for inviting me, but I have to be there anyway to invigilate it.

After prep, we gathered in the hall. One electric tube working, but her friends had done her proud. A top table was arranged with some sort of makeshift tablecloth, and chairs put in place. The honoured guests would sit there. I was kindly invited to sit at the top table, but declined and said I would sit at the back, it was their night, go and enjoy it.

The main party arrived, all done up to the nines (for each other). There was an MC, who was dressed in a suit and looked superb. It was more like a wedding reception than a birthday party. The rest of the guests sat on benches facing the stage.

The MC set the whole thing going. It began with a hymn (as usual, sung beautifully) and a prayer, a long, heartfelt prayer from one of her friends. Then the party.

There was a ten-minute sort of karaoke, with dancing, followed by singing.

Then the MC introduced the next 'act', which was three girls who sang unaccompanied very well; real modern rock stuff, followed by a brilliant song they composed themselves. Fantastic applause.

Then speeches, including one from a surrogate mother, who wished Stella all the best for the future with God's blessing and also said how proud she was of her. Then the cutting of the cake, and everyone was given a few crumbs and loved it (I, of course, was given a huge piece and a bottle of Coke, and the girls were too polite to share it with me when I tried to spread it around). I was then invited to have my photograph taken with the birthday girl. So much for being in the background.

There was great mirth and excitement and jollity, a real atmosphere, including a sort of bouncer who made sure only invited guests entered!

The MC introduced the second half, which was a repeat of the first half, with the same artists but different songs.

The MC made a speech thanking everybody. The party ended with another wonderful hymn and a long blessing and prayer.

I was very touched and immensely proud of the girls. They weren't cloying or precious, just plain lovely and beautiful, and so, so kind.

15.08.2005 Unruly Mob

Sudden, violent, terrifying and utterly, utterly ruthless. There is not a hint of pity or remorse or any human or humane reaction. It is just outright outrage. If a thief is caught in the act, mob rule takes over. He will be beaten to death, or kicked or stoned, or, even more probably and more horrifically, burned to death. This is achieved by either the use of a rubber necklace (a tyre around the neck set on fire) or putting him in a flour bag and dousing it with petrol.

Anne thinks it's the scapegoat syndrome. So many people are at thieving, including the participants of the lynch mob, that, when one is caught, it releases their pent-up frustration of anger and impotence and poverty. A sort of macabre ritual.

The nearest we have is football hooliganism, which is mindless and serves as some release to some inarticulate frustration and anger. But this is of a different order.

Last week, the girls found one thirteen or fourteen-year-old youth stealing their little bits of money and goods in one of the dorms. The accomplices were outside and weren't caught. The teachers arrived on the scene and were furiously angry, but, thank God, the police arrived and the boy escaped without a severe beating. It turns out he is part of a gang who steal everywhere, but the police even here are restrained in what they can do. It is frightening. Where the law doesn't protect you, the mob might. Dreadful thought.

Compare and Contrast

Last week, for St Clare's day, we had a concert. The enthusiasm and excitement were hugely high. The presentation left a little to be desired in professional terms, but it had bags of charm.

A line thrown across the stage; four sheets hung out as though drying, and this served as the stage curtain. Two people religiously pulled them back and forth whenever a scene or act changed, and some scenes lasted about one minute! The sketch was great; short but great. It was like a scene from a silent movie. The play, on AIDS, was interminable, and involved lots of clubbing and dancing and MELODRAMATIC dying. Oh, how they love to die in agony and pain! But their tradition is not oral or verse or written; it is not the word that holds sway: it is action. But the most amazing part is that in between acts or scenes, they had an eating competition (won, by the way, not by the male cook or some hefty girls, but by the smallest of the group) and musical chairs.

And there were lots of mime dances, i.e. a 'boy' and a girl dancing to modern music, and if the 'boy' acted and did boy stuff really well, the girls went into paroxysms of wild laughter.

A great afternoon of improbable and innocent pleasure.

03.09.2005 Outrage

Of course, what I am saying, bearing witness to, you already know.

You know how venal and corrupt Museveni is: you know more than me how he is strangling opposition, whose leaders or proponents are exiled or disappear; you know there is talk about the re-opening of the notorious torture rooms etc. You know all this. What violence awaits poor Uganda during the run-up to the elections, God only knows. But it is not of that I wish to speak. If the world can look on and remain mute whilst the madman Mugabe creates havoc for his own people, what chance has Uganda got?

No. I wish to talk about, rage against, the treatment, or maltreatment, of the north, and especially the Acholi tribe and the people of Gulu. Why is this man not dragged before the International Criminal Court? For twenty years, he has presided over their cultural and physical destruction. Yes, we know mad Phony Kony is the satanic rebel leader who abducts children and subjects them to heinous and disgusting rape and torture, turning them into 'soldiers' and murderers and sex slaves – of course he's nuts and satanic and evil – but those who allow the wanton and intentional destruction of a people are just as criminal. It is beyond belief that what the UN describes as the worst humanitarian crisis should draw so little attention and NO action.

Uganda is misleading because, with a name like 'Uganda', you can be seduced into thinking it is a country. It is a set of, a gathering of connecting tribes. As each leader, dictator, president takes power or office, so the star of his tribe rises. But it should not rise so far as to obliterate other tribes.

For twenty years, the war has raged. The so-called army, with its ghost soldiers (non-existent soldiers officers can claim wages for), is an occupying force. The soldiers routinely commit various crimes – murder, rape, robbery – and they have no sympathy with or for the populace of the north. Indeed, one minister was heard to say that the people of the north would make good fertiliser for the ground. It is like the hostility and enmity our tribes feel, the same antipathy or hate unionists feel for nationalists.

Over one million of these people live ('live' is not the word; exist) in these Internally Displaced Camps. Driven by the soldiers, in fear of execution if they stayed, they are huddled in these camps with food provided by the World Food Programme, and very inadequate sanitation, if any sanitation at all. Here reigns the culture of the flying toilet, so called because there are no latrines; people defecate in plastic bags and throw them away.

This once proud and prosperous people have been abandoned. They turn to alcoholism, sex (AIDS is rife) and despair; suicide can be alluring in this situation.

And the children. Those not in the camps trudge daily, in the morning and every night, for the shelter and safety and cold of the town and its shops and doorways and hospitals.

Twenty years. Twenty years!

It cries out to heaven; not for revenge, but for redress and for justice.

Something can and should be done about it. As I write, I hear about the awful tragedy of New Orleans. These neglected people will be helped because their plight is awful, but thankfully it is relatively short lived. As I write, I hear about those Sudanese who are flooding back to their homes despite the lack of food rather than staying in these prisons of despair called camps. And there is our answer. You know – you know better than I – but you must let the world know. It is your duty to tell the world.

There are wonderful people working in these camps. Get them to tell you. Get the latest statistics from the UN on rates of alcoholism, AIDS, death; on reported crimes committed by the army, on the number of suicides, on death spread by malaria and diseases spread by lack of sanitation. Get the facts; they are available.

Interest some producers in the BBC, or independent producers. Get them to film what is happening and use some subterfuge, saying you come to praise the old rascal or whatever. Show people what is going on. Give them a taste of real Reality TV.

It is a quiet, relentless tsunami. A gradual sort of genocide.
DO SOMETHING. Rescue these people. Save them.

When I return, I shall use every means at my disposal to bring to the attention of the world these people's suffering: the local media, the *Guardian*, local radio etc. Please let the politicians' energy and action make my intentions redundant by acting now.

22.09.2005   *Touching Rainbows*

'We saw crocodiles and buffalo and giraffes, and we touched a rainbow.' Helen's unforgettable phrase. And indeed she was right. On the top of Murchison Falls, the perfect arch of this wonderful rainbow was right next to us: wondrous, mystical.

Helen, Steve and Teresa, friends so close they are family, came out to see us and gave up their hard-earned holiday time to support us. That was very moving in itself (friendship is perhaps the most wonderful gift of all; happy the man who is friends with his children), but it also gave us the opportunity to explore other parts of Uganda with them. What an astonishingly beautiful, luxuriant and green land it is. No wonder Churchill called it 'the Pearl of Africa'.

First things first. They spent time at the school, having been exposed to the Alice-in-Wonderland experience of witnessing Kampala driving (boda-boda bikes are the Ugandan answer to kneecapping), and it allowed us to see our girls afresh. Well, they did themselves proud, as I knew they would. They were welcoming, enthusiastic and, at the welcome Mass, sang their hearts out in harmony. They put on a welcome show, did 'skits', danced traditional dances and mimed, performed a play, and one girl made a speech that would make a statue cry. They were great.

And Winnie. There are two Winnies. Must be the name. Winnie, our vivacious school cleaner, with four beautiful children and the outlook and exuberance of a seven-year-old, but who is very shy, did a whoopee welcome dance in the living room, no holds barred, with dancing to make King David thrill, embracing, ululating and a general 'come all ye'. Wow.

Winnie, the schoolgirl, composed, serious, responsible, whose face lights up like the Mona Lisa when she smiles, wrote a welcome song and sang it to them; artless, some would say, but charming and so warm.

Then we went to Murchison Falls National Game Park, up

the north-west; 3,840 square kilometres. We stayed at Para Lodge, and the view from the balcony of our window alone was worth the money; the Nile meandering swiftly, majestically, as it has done since before Moses was a boy.

But then, at 7 a.m., Frank, our driver, and Henry, our game warden, took us for our game drive. 'On a clear day, rise and look around you. How it will astound you, the beauty you see... You can see forever and ever more.' The composer must have been to the park. The vastness of it, the silent explosion of it, the infinitely changing vegetation, the open, endless, endless sky; it was a Teilhard de Chardin experience. You could feel and sense nature growing, living. And the astonishing birds, the variety and colour: the red bishop, the black and white kingfisher, the snake brown eagle and a host of others. All combined, sight and sound, to overwhelm you and subdue you and humble you. Oh, yes, the lion and elephants and the superior giraffe were great to see, but the real star was the savannah itself.

Next to that, a different but impressive vista was the gardens at Kingfisher Nile in Jinja; 95% nature, 5% intervention, the owner told me. More controlled, but the cocoa nut tree, the palm trees, the bushes and stunningly beautiful flowers, all against the setting of the Nile, with fishermen boating and fishing as they did thousands of years ago.

If Uganda finds unity and stability and can be mature enough to throw off parasitical corruption, it would have a great future and serve its people brilliantly.

22.09.2005 Forgive Us Our Trespasses

To walk humbly. I am astonished, humbled, mystified, rather as when you read a part of the gospel that you've read a thousand times before, but suddenly the meaning hits you; it is outrageous. Many of the sayings, commands of Jesus go against everything else that nature and culture endow us with or teach us. They just defy logic – and yet, without them, we cannot be his followers.

Take 'forgiveness': the very heart of Christianity. It is even the central part of the prayer we have been instructed to pray – but it violates every instinct and every law of civilisation. 'Forgive'?

Our (the West's) legal system is punitive. Of course, so is the African legal system. Our media scream at us to 'lock up the bastards and throw away the key' whenever we capture someone who commits a dastardly crime: child abuser, terrorist, murderer, rapist – and yes, I admit, I am just as bloodthirsty and hot for revenge. But I am wrong.

I have told before of the horrific instant mob justice carried out if the Africans – or at least the Ugandans – catch a thief. But, if they don't catch him and punish him immediately, the African culture is not punitive, not revenge-seeking, but deeper, there is a culture too of reconciliation and healing. This is, perhaps, most eloquently exemplified in the peace and reconciliation process that took place in South Africa, but it is part of the African culture, practice and instinct generally.

We have a group, blasphemously called 'the Lord's Resistance Army' – each word a misnomer – which carries out the worst atrocities imaginable against little ones and their parents; 'satanic', I have heard them described as. My instinct is to hunt them down and kill them. They are irredeemable in my eyes. But the people who have been persecuted by them for twenty years would prefer to be reconciled, to invite them back into the fold. Amazing. Stupefying. Beyond reason.

But then the gospel is beyond reason. Jesus and the cross are beyond reason. Reason, in one way, has nothing to do with it – except that, if you are reconciled, if you do bring them back into the fold, then they will become productive and their humanity will be restored. That is reasonable.

Our 'civilisation' and its relentless punitive measurements may well have it wrong. No. It does have it wrong. This pre-Christian African way is more profound, more Christian, than any in the West.

The quality of mercy.

04.10.2005 Power to the People

Sometimes it is like living on a yoyo. The power goes off at 7 p.m. We all think it is 'load shedding': the process in which they cut off the electricity for three or four hours because they don't generate enough for the whole country (they do supply Kenya in a deal in which they sell at a loss, but Kenya's supplies are never cut off – don't ask!). The next day, I phone the manager, whose name is (I swear I am not making this up) Mr Ojoke. Ojoke by name and nature.

'Oh.'

The next day, I phone again.

'Oh, yes, someone else phoned.'

That afternoon: 'The man who looks at the poles missed it.' The town didn't miss it, but he did.

The next day: 'The lorry broke down in the yard. We're borrowing one from the next district.'

'THE lorry broke down?'

'No, the one with the poles on.'

That afternoon, Wednesday: 'Worse than we thought, the transformer needs replacing.'

'When will that be done?'

'Not before Monday.'

'Monday! Five days!'

Monday: 'We are trying to get it, we are on our way.'

Eventually, after twelve days, power is restored – for one and a half hours! Altogether, 297 hours without electricity.

But the loss of power has other implications. After some time, the water, running tap water, goes. That means flushing the loos is a problem. For macho types out there, it would call for a toss of the head and complete indifference. For pampered weaklings like me, it calls for what can only be described as panic. But you do adapt and become ingenious and economical with the precious stuff called water.

Yes, for drinking and cups of tea: bottled. For bathing: get your gerry can, fill the pan, boil, place in basin that is in the bath, put three times the cold water into the boiling water, get in the bath, bathe all over, and use the water for filling the cistern for flushing the loo. Clever, what! And the funny thing is, you get used to it and just do it. But when the water returns! Ah, the pleasure, luxury, of washing your hands instead of applying the antiseptic gel etc... heaven.

When I become dictator... but we have one of those already.

04.10.2005 Hell

To describe the kitchen. No, not kitchen; the place, or hellhole, where food is cooked. And to describe the long-suffering cooks.

The blackened, very blackened, almost-door leads into an area of five metres by four metres. The walls are incredible, almost beyond saving: black, grimy, with enough burnt stuff impressed into the very fabric as to be virtually irremovable.

About the space are three 'missionary' pots or ovens – the sort we used to see in cartoons with missionaries being boiled alive. Only now, it is posho and beans. Two of the three do not work, and none have chimneys that work, so the cooks work in a maze of perpetual smoke that smarts the eyes and does God knows what to the lungs. There is, of course, not a tap or any sort of washing-up facility to be seen.

So things are about to be changed.

In the holidays, two new ovens, with fixed, working chimneys, on a platform of tiles are to be installed. The walls are to be scraped and whitewashed. Water for washing is (somehow) to be put in place. Outside, there are to be sinks for the children to wash their plates.

If you are trying to instil in these wonderful kids a sense of their own dignity and worth, c'mon, let's face it, you have to start with their living conditions and environment. Which is why we are bidding for a grant to give them dormitories that are safe and inviting, rather than army barracks, crammed with heaving bodies, with no fire escape. They will also get more toilets – inside – and tanks to provide water for their showers. That's the grant.

But the kitchen is coming from the money we raised. And it shall indeed raise; not only the working conditions of our three merry cooks, but the standard of hygiene and sense of well-being among the kids.

The three cooks, Lawrence, Margaret and Kamu – pronounced just like the French author Camus – well, they deserve a chapter all of their own. Amazing.

14.10.2005 Dear Emma...

Dear Emma, Heather and Hazel (and, of course, Maggie),

I thought I would write to you a little about our school so that you could get a 'feel' for it, and see the differences and the things that are the same. Yes, there are differences, but the girls are girls, exactly the same as you, with all the hobbies and excitements and exasperations and delights and worries of every other girl all over the world. They are a delight to be with (most of the time, but they too have their moments!).

I thought I would give you a run-down of their day.

Well, first of all it is a boarding school, and it is a very Spartan, that is tough, existence. I shall send you a photograph of the girls and you will notice that they all have short or shaven hair. It is a school rule for hygiene and for making sure that girls don't waste time on frivolities. I bet that would go down well in your school! There has been great excitement because I bought them an electric razor to shave their heads, which they love; before, they had to use a comb and ordinary razor blade, which they hated because it hurt them. Now they are delighted.

Of course, they sleep at school. Their dorms. Well, again, they are thrilled, because we bought every girl in the school a mosquito net. You can't believe the difference it has made. Before, the girls frequently got malaria, and malaria is the biggest disease and killer here, even though there are other awful diseases. We haven't got rid of it completely, but the rate of infection has drastically dropped.

At the moment, we are in the bidding process with the wonderful Irish government (and I mean it; the Irish government is very generous to poor countries) to get the dorms upgraded. These are young secondary school girls, and sixty or seventy are squashed into one long room (there are four dorms) with no space and NO fire escape! I am fighting that.

So they get to bed at 10.30 p.m. for seniors, 10 p.m. for

juniors. They get up at 5.30 a.m. and wash in the shower rooms. Don't be fooled by the word 'shower'. Each girl gets a gerry can and basin of cold water, goes to the concrete shower cubicle and washes.

Then straight to 'prep', which is what you and I would call study or homework.

7 A.M.	Breakfast, which consists of a 'drink' of porridge – not like ours.
7.20 A.M.	General clean-up.
7.40 A.M.	General prayers and announcements.
8 A.M.–1 P.M.	Classes.
1 P.M.	Lunch, which consists of posho – a sort of tasteless mashed potato and beans – not baked beans – every day except Sunday. On Sunday they get one piece of meat and rice.
2–4 P.M.	Classes.
4–6 P.M.	Showers and clubs.
6–7 P.M.	Dinner. The same as lunch, except on Wednesday they get sweet potatoes.
7–9.30 P.M. OR 10 P.M.	'Prep' again.

As I said, it is a hard regime, and yet the girls are so cheerful, so full of fun. And they love singing and they love dancing, and (thank God) they love jokes, even my jokes. I wish you could meet them. Anyway, you shall see them, because I am taking over a little piece of film I took of them. They are great.

Of course, some of them have heart-breaking stories. One bad practice over here is polygamy: some of their fathers have several wives, which means sometimes the children are abandoned. But that's another story. They consider themselves lucky because they are at school, and they so want to learn.

Anyway, I thought you'd like to know how your counterparts live. Your family and friends have made a huge difference to their lives and you should be very proud of them. For example, not only do we have many, many more books, but we have a computer suite with eleven computers and we are on the Internet – something unimaginable a couple of years ago. There are all sorts of improvements to the school. And next year we plan to start vocational courses, like catering, beauty courses – hairdressing etc. – and, very importantly, agriculture. It's all very exciting. If that takes off, I'll get you all over here so you can have a hair do; I promise you won't have to be shaven!

Good luck at your school!

Seamus

PS Over here they use my second name because they can't say Seamus, so I am Patrick!

14.10.2005 Moments in School Life

Going over to the rosary and passing Harriet (a lovely, ever-cheerful girl), who catches my eye, offers half her guava, says, 'God says what little you have, share' and bursts into peals of laughter. Magic.

The girls return from a day, or half-a-day, visit to a National Park – the first outing they have been on, full of excitement and infectious glee, jumping up and down. A treat. A treat. An unlooked-for, unexpected prize, but prized above, far above, its worth. The joy on their faces. The haste to capture the feeling by taking 'snaps'. Whoopee.

And in our counselling group. Barbara, haltingly, hauntingly, telling of her abandonment by her father because he's married a new young bride the same age as her. To please his new bride, Barbara is rejected, discarded, doubt even cast on her legitimacy ('I don't even know if you are really mine'). Quiet heaving; tears flowing. How can you fill that void, heal that hurt? But that story is repeated all over the world.

Cinderella

We are doing *Cinderella*, but we have decided to do it African style. Of course, we have Cinderella and the stepmother, but this is Africa, so she has ten stepmothers. And she doesn't go to the ball in a carriage, but on a boda-boda bike. And, as well as the fairy godmother, we also have a witch doctor. Oh, if only you could witness the witch doctor's performance. If Spielberg ever sees or hears of her, she's made her fortune. What a girl. The whole cast roll around in laughter, and that is in rehearsal. Get a plane, buy a ticket, come and see her; she's worth it.

Uganda

One of our young teachers comes to see me. She has a problem. If ever anyone needs help, they utter the same mantra: 'I have a problem.' She had not done any of her duties for two days, and I was ready to look hurt and remonstrate and talk about professionalism. The problem is this: although she looks about thirteen, she is married, with two young children. Like everyone over here, she has a house girl, and the house girl has run away; she is missing. One of the neighbours says she has been hanging around with a boy and they think they've done a Romeo and Juliet.

The father of the girl arrives and says she was the teacher's responsibility and accuses her of selling the girl for child sacrifice: a charming little practice still in occasional use over here. The teacher vehemently denies the charge. The father reports her to the police, which is where I come in. The police are willing to drop the case if she pays them 100,000 shillings; in our terms a hundred quid, but the exchange rate is forty quid. She is short of 30,000 shillings. I lend, case is dropped, end of story. Well, end of story so far.

Will the police look for the girl? Of course not. Will the father look for the girl? Now, that remains to be seen.

14.10.2005 The World Revolves around the...

Wheel. Bicycles. Bikes. The place and importance of bicycles in the developing countries cannot be over-estimated or imagined. They are the means of transport, a source of income and a matter of pride. The number of bikes we pass on the way to the local town are beyond count. And what they carry on their bikes is beyond belief: livestock, sugar cane, beds, furniture, charcoal, maize, coffins (empty – I think) and, of course, people. People old, young, men, women (side-saddle), children, sober, drunk, happy, sad, awake or asleep. These 'boda-boda' bicycle taxi guys are what we call *'kanyama'*, which means 'tough guy', strong, macho guy, and, boy, are they. How they are, when you consider the laws of physics and biology, is a complete mystery – their diet is practically non-existent, except for posho and beans – but tough they are; as tough as oxen. That is extraordinary.

But even more extraordinary is another group of cyclists. Because of the poor diet, or lack of health care or pre-natal care, there are a disproportionate number of people with spina bifida or other crippling diseases. This allows the introduction of a new member of the 'bike' family: the hand bike. It is a bicycle that is pedalled by hand, for those who have no use in their legs. And do they go at a pace! If the boda-boda guys are *'kanyama'*, I would not like to take these guys on in arm wrestling. These machines are a wonderful invention, affording the user complete independence and restoring their dignity and self-esteem. Whoever invented it deserves a Nobel Prize for services to humanity. Ah, pedal power. More power to your elbow

Mind you, they behave with the same rigorous attention to the rules of the road as the rest of Ugandans; i.e. if there are any, they totally and blithely ignore them. At night, no cyclist would ever think of having lights on his bike (and here there are no street lights), and it is part of the game to make those rich buggers who can afford cars be constantly alert and nervous wrecks. Not the

Ugandan driver, however, who is incapable of even thinking that anyone else on the road has any rights. Indeed, no one else should be on the road. So, whether it is single file, two abreast, three abreast, overtaking on a bend without hand signals or allowances of any kind, bicycle or car, it matters not. This is life in the fast lane (and death, too).

20.10.2005 Gulu Walk

Gulu. A town. A town like any other town. A town unlike any other town in Uganda; in the world.

A town is home to residents, shopkeepers, hoteliers, hospitals, businessmen, banks, markets, pubs, schools, colleges, churches, libraries. So is Gulu; but it is also a home to, a refuge for, thousands and thousands of fleeing, frightened, weary, worn-out children and adults called 'commuters', Night after night, relentlessly, with no break, no let-up, no holiday, they trudge their way to Gulu, tramping their way to doorways, hospital entrances, church steps, makeshift camps, streets for protection, for security. They are driven by fear: fear of kidnap, mutilation, abduction, death. Their lives and minds have been darkened, invaded by the madness and evil of malicious war and unsparing bleak horror.

This is their life. For many, the only life they have known. The children do not run to their shelter; they do not skip, or play games, or laugh, but grimly, joylessly, walk to Gulu.

Tonight, we are here to remember the people of Gulu. We are here to join with them, to be one with them in their suffering by calling it to mind, and to ask God our Father to move men's hearts and minds and resolutions, that the people of Gulu may be spared and may be relieved of their suffering.

We shall have readings from scripture.

We shall have periods of silence. We shall have meditations when we tell stories of a man, a woman, a child, to try to imagine what the people are going through.

We shall pray, for we are all one. Uniting ourselves in prayer to the Lord Jesus, who is one with them, we too shall be one with them, our brothers and sisters of Gulu.

God, our Father, is never indifferent to his children's suffering. He is with them at their darkest moment. The cries of infants, the sobbing of mothers, the despair of fathers are witnessed and shared by Him. He saw his own Son, disowned, tortured and butchered.

1 READING: ISAIAH 53:3[1]

A man of sorrows, acquainted with grief.

Reflection

THE WOMAN'S TALE

The sun is about to leave us; leave us to darkness and danger. Now, I must stop what I am doing, tidy my place, and pray and hope it will still be here tomorrow – not burned down or ransacked or robbed, like my father's was. Wearily, I gather the children, I call. They do not run to me, but come listlessly. I have stopped looking into their eyes, their lifeless eyes. Then, without eagerness, without feeling, we set out. We walk. We walk the same route every night. We walk the same route every morning. We meet the same people and join the same line, the long, long line of the slow-moving army of 'commuters'. It is a strange name for those driven out by fear. We snake our way to town, to a hard doorway, open to the weather, to the wind, to the rain, to the whims of fortune, to look for safety and, if we are lucky, unconsciousness. It is only in unconsciousness, in oblivion that the weariness, the dreariness, the fatigue and exhaustion can be forgotten. We do not sleep; or, if we sleep, we sleep fitfully, snatching a few moments here and there. And when we wake, we wake in fear. Fear is our second skin.

Morning.
Dawn.
No relief.
No joy.
We begin to walk.

Prayer

> God Our Father,
> Bless and be with all the mothers of Gulu in their
> suffering and pain. Give them the strength to carry
> on. May our mother Mary give them comfort and

---

[1] All Bible references are to the Revised Standard Version.

peace of mind. And may they soon be able to dare to hope. We ask this through Jesus Our Lord.

2 READING: LAMENTATIONS 1 and 2:9–12

How lonely sits the city
That was full of people!
How like a widow she has become,
She that was great among the nations!
She that was a princess among the cities
Has become a vassal.

She weeps bitterly in the night,
Tears on her cheeks;
Among her lovers
She has none to comfort her;
All her friends have dealt treacherously with her,
They have become her enemies.

The roads to Zion mourn,
For none come to the appointed feasts;
All her gates are desolate,
Her priests groan,
Her maidens have been dragged away
And she herself suffers bitterly.

All her people groan
As they search for bread;
They trade their treasure for food
To revive their strength.
'Look, O Lord, and behold,
For I am despised.

Is it nothing to you, all who pass by?
Look and see
If there is any sorrow like to my sorrow
Which was brought upon me.'

The elders of the daughters of Zion
Sit on the ground in silence;
They have cast dust on their heads
And put on sackcloth;
The maidens of Jerusalem
Have bowed their heads to the ground.

My eyes are spent with weeping;
My soul is in tumult;
My heart is poured out in grief
Because of the destruction of the
Daughter of my people,
Because infants and babes faint
In the streets of the city.

They cry to their mothers,
'Where is bread and wine?'
As they faint like wounded men
In the streets of the city
As their life is poured out
On their mothers' bosom.

This is the word of the Lord

Reflection

THE CHILD'S TALE

Such a long way. Such a long, long way.

I do not like going. I do not like the doorway where we sleep. It stinks. I am always hungry. I am always thirsty.

Rita is my sister. She is old. She is nine. She looks after me. She is kind. She protects me. Sometimes she is harsh with me; if I cry. She does not like me crying.

But sometimes I am cold. Sometimes I am hungry. And sometimes... sometimes I am frightened.

The big people, the grown-ups, do not talk to me. They do not talk to Rita. They just... look.

One day, Rita says, we will be able to stay at home. One day.

She always says that.
We never do.

Prayer

O God Our Father,
Bless and protect and give warmth and comfort to the children of the north. May they know that they are not forgotten or abandoned. Give them peace and rest soon.
We ask this through Jesus Our Lord.
God will never desert His people, no matter how long or dreadful their suffering. He remains with them, and will, in time, out of time, wipe away every tear and heal every wound. Let us listen to what Paul says.

3 READING: ROMANS 8:35

Who shall separate us from the love of Christ?
Shall trouble or hardship or persecution or
famine or nakedness or danger or sword?

Reflection

THE MAN'S TALE

Once I had land; much land. Good land; fertile and rich. Once I had cattle and goats and hens. Then they chased me away. They drove me from my home. They said, if I stayed, I would give help and shelter to the rebels. I would be a rebel and they would shoot me. They drove me from my land, my ancestral land. They took away my land,
My living,
My history,
My culture,
My dignity.

My life.

Once I was a farmer; now I am a refugee – in my own country.

I grew food; now I beg food.

Once I measured my life by the seasons; now by the bottle.

Once my children looked to me; now they look past me.

Once I held my head up among my people; now it is held down.

Once I was rich; now I am poor.

Once I was a man, a father, a husband; now... I am nothing.

Once I thought I would leave my children good land, a large inheritance, a history, a culture.

Now our history is written in blood on the pages of despair, our culture desecrated and destroyed. Look what I bequeath them now; this squeezed, squashed, screwed-up piece of space. I bequeath them squalor, hunger, filth, disease, hopelessness and death.

Prayer

> O God our Father,
> Have pity and come to the aid of the fathers of Gulu. Change men's hearts of stone into hearts of flesh, that they may recognise their suffering, restore their dignity and land, and give them fresh hope.
> We ask this through Jesus Our Lord.
> We are with the people of Gulu. We weep at their suffering. We pray earnestly for them.
> But we are the body of Christ. It is through our efforts, our strength, our courage that God's kingdom shall be established on Earth. Each of us can play our part in bringing this suffering to an end. Each of us must play her part, whether it is prayer or using whatever gifts we have at our disposal; must bring the plight of our people to the attention of the world, and ask, demand, insist that their suffering must end.
> For what sort of society does our Father want? He does not, nor we, want revenge. We do not want

more bloodshed. We want a cessation of war, a restoration of peace, and a reconciliation between peoples. We pray that the psalmist's song comes true:

> Mercy and truth have embraced;
> Justice and Peace will kiss.

Let us finally listen to what Paul has to say about how we should live, we here at St Clare's.

4 READING: PHILIPPIANS 2:1–11

> If there is any encouragement in Christ, any solace in love, any participation in the Spirit, any compassion and mercy,
> Complete my joy by being of the same mind, with the same united love, united in heart, thinking one thing.
> Do nothing out of selfishness or vainglory; rather humbly, regard others as more important than yourselves,
> Each looking out not for his own interests, but also everyone for those of others.
>
> Have among yourselves the same attitude that is also yours in Christ Jesus,
> Who, though he was in the form of God, did not regard equality with God something to be grasped.
> Rather, he emptied himself, taking the form of a slave, coming in human likeness;
> And found human in appearance, he humbled himself, becoming obedient unto death, even the death on the cross.
> Because of this, God has greatly exalted him and bestowed upon him the name that is above every name,

> That at the name of Jesus every knee should bend, of those in heaven and on earth and under the earth,
> And every tongue confess that Jesus Christ is Lord, to the Glory of God the Father.

Reflection

We shall go in silence from this place and pray that the Spirit of God, the Giver of Life, the bestower of Peace and Courage and Wisdom and Love, be in our hearts and minds and remains with us.

Prayer

> We pray Lord that we live our loves as St Paul encourages us to do: to live to serve each other in love.

24.10.2005 Gulu Walk Two

What a day. What a walk.

I travelled down from Budaka, which takes about three and a half hours. I joke not: it is the one and only time I have been overtaken by a hearse with a coffin in, draped in a sort of net covering, the driver weaving in and out of traffic at speed! It must have been the guy who was late for his own funeral.

We arrived at Makere University, whence the walk started. I have a sort of radar or emit some signal or scent that sends out messages to every sort of loon or weirdo to come and pester me. I attract nutters. This chap was from the west of Uganda, and very smartly dressed he was. He was a 'born again'. I have nothing against people being born again; I have a little difficulty working out why they were born in the first place. With one exception, the ones I have met here have been rogues and cheats every one. Jesus had sent me to meet this fellow; it was part of his divine plan, he assured me. Within half an hour, he had asked me to send him Bibles because he was a preacher. Then did I know that to preach the word, preachers needed financial support? When this received less than rapturous applause, he told me that, on the way to the walk, he had been robbed of every worldly possession. Then, when he found out I was a teacher, his family had property; would I go and run a school for them? I told him I was already working.

But this is the side show. Every event has a side show.

The walk itself. Magnificent. Mainly young people, with a good peppering of *msungus* (white people; so should that be a good salting?) The speakers were first class, and the sound system – wow. There were people from all sorts of organisations: the Red Cross, UNICEF, World Vision and a host of NGOs. Almost everyone was Ugandan. Oh, and a pop star with an incredible voice, who recorded a special song for the children of Gulu. Outstanding. If they played that enough, the war would soon end.

And there were traditional dancers and musicians from Gulu. You just have to see it to believe it. Wow, how they move!

The speakers were universally good: passionate, articulate, and experienced in the awful, dreadful plight of the people of Gulu. We marched to outside Parliament, which has been deaf to the cries of the children of Gulu for twenty years.

We heard the facts recited like a litany: twenty-four thousand children abducted to be made soldiers or mules or sex slaves; countless people mutilated and murdered; all of the people disinherited and thrown off their land etc., etc. But the one real sadness for the organisers was that, in Uganda, only two cities were walking: Kampala and Gulu. Forty cities all over the world, from Beijing to Washington (and, of course, Coventry!). Did Ugandans not realise, when a northern Ugandan died, it was a brother or sister who died?

But the mood of the walk was good natured and good humoured. There were about 300–400 people; small by Western standards, but, I am told, good for Uganda. We marched with a happy, loud, full-of-life brass band, and brass bands in the open air are just good for the spirit, soul and heart.

However, there was one unforgettable moment. They had a boy and a girl from Gulu: night walkers, 'commuters'. The girl told of the difficulties facing the youngsters: finding a safe place to sleep; the impossibility of being able to study because of the walking; easy prey for rape from boda-boda boys or sugar daddies. Awful.

Then Patrick spoke. Patrick, I imagine, is about twelve, though these kids have been through so much, it is hard to tell. He spoke clearly, if just a little quickly, in his artless way, with his piping voice. Then he suddenly said, without warning, 'I want to tell you a story. When they took us (meaning when he and his brothers and sisters were abducted), they made us murder our mother and father.' And he abruptly stopped. There was a moment, an eternal moment, when you felt, rather than heard, his suppressed sob; for that instant, he lost control of his features, and briefly his face crumbled. Then he wiped away his tears, turned and sat down. He could not go on. And in that moment, we glimpsed the full horror that had been visited upon this child, the full evil.

I wish we could all walk to Gulu. I wish there were some way we could pick up every one of those twenty-four thousand children, and hug the warmth and love of life back into them. I wish this bloody government would protect its young, instead of abandoning them. The whole world should march to Gulu.

17.11.2005 Slip Sliding Away

There is a horrible fascination about watching a country, society, a loose connection of tribes, however you describe Uganda, sliding into the abyss, becoming an overt fascist state. All the pieces are there before you, but you fail to see the 'gestalt', the pattern, until it is too late.

The endemic level of corruption is astounding; in every phase of public and private life it is there. And everyone gets away with it. The most corrupt, of course, must be Museveni, the president. When you begin to itemise his possessions and power and abuse of power, you are left gasping.

When Museveni came out of the bush, he had nothing; but he had a long memory and a desire for revenge. It is claimed that he prosecutes or allows the war in the north to be prosecuted as a punishment for not supporting him against Obote. And the list of crimes committed there is chilling. Nearly two million people driven off their land and shoved into Internally Displaced Camps, which, considering their conditions, are akin to concentration camps, where despair, disease, alcoholism, AIDS, STDs, hunger are rife. And the president's brother runs all sorts of scams, using forced labour and robbing the owners of their land for his own profit.

It is, of course, well documented by the Human Rights group that the army, which is supposed to be there to protect them, is an occupying force, committing crimes of rape, torture and murder with impunity. The army again runs all sorts of shady deals, from paying 'ghost' soldiers to purchasing below-standard equipment and arms from unofficial sources, having creamed off a fair whack for themselves.

But it's the people who are the victims of this callous indifference. They have lost their land, their livelihood, their dignity, their way of life because it is profitable for a few gangsters. And they must be punished. It is a sort of cultural genocide. When they do disperse the camps, more aid will be called for, and the aid will go straight into the waiting arms of the same gangsters, including, of course, Al Capone Museveni.

Museveni is now fast becoming the new Mugabe.

One measure of a fascist state is how it treats its press, or the freedom of the press. Museveni is paranoid about criticism. One journalist has frequently criticised the president over, for example, having eighty (I joke not) advisers and more soldiers to guard him than do the 1.8 million people in the camps. He also is puzzled by why the president needs a private jet, which cost millions of dollars and which costs a fortune to maintain, when the hospitals have no drugs and the infrastructure is falling to bits. Oh, and he also used it to ferry his daughter to Germany to give birth because he does not trust Ugandan doctors! For this, the journalist was thrown in prison and is on ten charges of 'sedition'.

Opponents disappear, or are tortured, or mysteriously die.

He may have gone a little too far this time with his arresting of the opposition leader on trumped-up charges. I hear that even our local lads who say they used to rig the vote for him in the previous elections will no longer do so. His lust for power remains undimmed, however, and, with feelings running high, and an army that is ruthless and armed, and commanders threatening dire consequences for anyone who opposes the 'commander in chief', you can sadly see the road ahead. The people will indeed be eating bread of tears.

So why, why, why do our governments continue to support this rotten regime? Why are they pouring endless money into the pockets of these greedy, rapacious, mendacious gangsters? They have intelligent men on the ground. They read the reports of the UN, of the Human Rights groups, of the Global Fund findings; so why?

We need an investigative reporter. We need a Fergus Keane. We need someone with a camera and a nose for getting to the truth and exposing this madness. Oh, I know this is just another story among countless stories of greed and corruption, but does it have to be propped up by our governments? Let us tell the regime here that we are sick of the stench of this sewer. Let us serve the poor, not their overlords and masters.

Latest

Like all bizarre events, it mixes high comedy, Keystone Kops comedy, with terror. Fourteen of the co-accused along with the opposition leader, Besigye, were granted bail. Besigye was not granted bail. Immediately, a newly-formed force, known as the Black Mambas or, believe it or not, the Men in Black, armed with guns at the ready, surrounded the courtroom and tried to intimidate the crowd and seize the released prisoners to take them to a secret location. As someone in the crowd said, it is the return of Amin. There were disputes between the prison guards and these Men in Black, but eventually the released got away in a bus. Fascism rules OK.

I quote from today's non-governmental newspaper, *The Daily Monitor*, which they are threatening to close down:

> For the past twenty years, donors have created this opportunistic culture of permissiveness using Museveni as a pawn in the region. They have left violations of human rights unanswered, skirted Uganda's culpability in the DRC massacres and use of violence in domestic elections.
>
> They continue to pump millions of dollars into the economy, ignoring reports of corruption, cronyism, influence peddling and outright graft. Ahead of this week's inferno, the World Bank approved a 130 million dollar aid package to Uganda, claiming that we met performance targets in several critical areas including governance.
>
> The Global Fund jumped at the appointment of the Judicial Commission, a chance to continue a 300 million dollar programme while patients in hospital go without drugs.

24.11.2005 *Cosmic Cosmas*

She looked amazing. She has the power still to astonish. She moves at lightning pace; her mind as active and busy as Einstein's, and her commitment to the slum children with whom she still works undiminished. Sister Cosmas. Prayer and work, and a huge dose of humour. What a girl!

Last week, we celebrated her eightieth birthday. Twelve of us (all the congregation came) went to a Belgian restaurant. There are very few things that delight as much as the sight of a beautifully laid-out table, with soft napkins, tablecloths, sparkling wine glasses and cutlery – ah, perfect. Sister looked radiant, in a dark greenish-brown suit and her nun's headscarf (you can't really call them wimples), her eyes shining, just delighting in the setting, the company (her family, really), the food and the atmosphere.

The meal was excellent. People had a range of things, from peppered steaks to beer casserole (me) and mashed potatoes, to pan-fried chicken with peaches and vegetarian meals. Delicious. And, of course, wine.

For the sweet, we had had a Belgian chocolate birthday cake with Cosmas's name inscribed and the number '80' displayed made by the chef, which went well with her sticker she was wearing, saying 'The best eighty-year-old around'.

If you think that was good, on the following Tuesday, Cosmas, Sister Maureen (the wonderful Maureen) and Anne and I were invited to the Irish Ambassador's residence for dinner. I had informed them it was Sr Cosmas's eightieth and that she had been in Africa, serving the poor, serving as a highly esteemed and loved teacher at other times for fifty-six years. Fifty-six years! The Ambassador came up trumps, and was delighted to honour Cosmas with this dinner. Cosmas was so pleased and delighted to be thus recognised.

Two speeches, sermons, whatever, moved me. The priest, African priest, Fr David, celebrated Mass for Cosmas on her birthday. Everyone should have the opportunity to assist at his Masses. He speaks so movingly. He is so excited about the love of God, God's tender love for us, that it pours out of him. He created a beautiful image. He kept saying that no one is born by accident, none of us is here by mistake, we are the children of a loving father. But his image was that Cosmas's heart had been beating for eighty years, and every beat was a pulse of God's love. Making the heart beat with that love.

The other was Cosmas's little thank you at the beginning of the dinner at the Ambassador's residence, in reply to her charming speech. Cosmas thanked God for her life, but especially for all the people she had met, and how, while she greatly loved and above all admired them all, she held in the highest esteem the African women, their dignity, their facing up to almost impossible odds, their mutual support, their courage. She spoke with such wonder and conviction.

It never ceases to amaze me. When I think of where she came from: obviously from a very loving home, with adored father and mother and deeply loved siblings, but the atmosphere of the church in Ireland in those days; it was not so much Mother Church as Stepmother Church. It was often an organ of repression and power, and yet this church sent out the most amazing missionaries: men and women full of love and service, who, literally, transformed Africa, and the face and future of so many countless people. The love of these men and women still courses through the veins of the people. They still speak of them with such love and affection. 'Paradox' is hardly the word.

I am forever grateful that I have had the opportunity to meet these women: these ordinary extraordinary people. I love them and am proud to call them friends.

When I grow up, I'm going to become a nun!

29.11.2005 Shall We Dance?

Now and again you are taken completely by surprise.

The prison conditions over here, I am led to believe, leave a lot to be desired. Suffice it to say, you would not want to spend your holidays there. Images of *Midnight Express* come to mind.

Yesterday, I met a revered and noble man who is well into his late seventies, but, as is often the case, a man of mental agility and still physically able and fit. He is a retired C of E priest, who served many parishes in England, but who also laboured for ten years in West Africa. He is here visiting retired clergymen and their widows, to enquire after their well-being. He is appalled and agitated to find that these people are just abandoned (as are so many in Uganda), without a pension or, indeed, any provision whatsoever. It is a scandal. Abandoned by what he calls 'the living Church'. I don't know what, but I am sure he will do something about it.

He told a marvellous story of an encounter he has had on his short visit. One retired clergyman decided, now that his responsibilities were served and completed, to offer his time and service to the women's prison. Over two years, he had gathered a band of fourteen (five female, nine male) volunteer prison visitors. He went to see the prison. He expected at least Holloway.

On entering, the warden received them; he and the volunteer chaplain. She proclaimed, Alleluia, that she was a Christian, and the six prisoners around the table were her children. They then went to a chapel across the courtyard, where a larger group met, and they had some sort of liturgical service, with great singing and dancing, with which the guards joined in. There was much singing, dancing, clapping, high spirits and joyous, happy praise.

The warden claims it was all because this retired vicar started his mission, including her conversion.

It makes you think about how you treat people etc. Heart warming.

Heart Chilling

A story that is not so warming. I told you about Sr Cosmas. She is still working with one nursery in the slums, and in the slums you really are talking poverty big style. Three weeks ago, one of the two-and-a-half-year-olds was kidnapped, which immediately sparked off panic and a manhunt. Even slum people, or some of them, contacted radios or community radios. The message was broadcast over the radio and everyone was on the lookout. There was a panic because a new big building was being erected in a nearby, affluent part of town, and the custom in this country is to sacrifice a child and put him/her in the foundations to bring good luck. Grisly, unbelievable, but a common practice.

The search was so immediate, and the alarm set off so early, that people reported seeing a boy here, and later there with this guy etc. The child was found, thank God, two and a half days later. He is safe, but Sister says she is not sure about well. How long does it take to get over a trauma like that? Without professional counselling or care? Hopefully, his carers, father or mother or grandmother will nurture him back to full health. Well done, the community!

Going Home

We have had to send the girls home a week early, just in case, because of the political upheaval. It is so eerie without them. It brings home how cheerful and lovely they are. Of course, half the time you could strangle some of the beggars, but only for a second, because they are special. Anyway, they are gone. The empty feeling is like going to a fancy restaurant and the place being deserted; it is a feeling of alienation instead of good fellowship.

Last stuff from Africa this year. Going home to see if I can shake a few bones to get the big people interested in the plight of the north and Uganda as a whole; you know, the politicians etc. Wish me luck.

PS By the way, we are just in that season. All my Ugandan friends are saying, 'Ah! Too hot!'

08.03.2006 *Disasters and Delights*

A curious few days; full of the extraordinary and banal.

The extraordinary. Travelling on the way to Mbale, the local 'big' town, I noticed that a crash barrier was buckled badly. Then the head told me the story. A lorry, travelling at night, as some do (though very dangerous, since there are no streetlights); travelling at speed, as they all do; its lights failed. The driver veered off the road, dislodging his heavy load of barrels full of molasses. The two men on top, his 'boys' to help him unload, were thrown, and the barrels fell on top of them. As always in these circumstances, the driver fled, never to be seen again. One 'boy' was killed instantly; the other was in great agony but died soon after. Although it was pitch black, in the dead of night, the local villagers came to help. It must also be said that, if there were anything worth robbing, they would have availed themselves of the opportunity.

The authorities got involved, and what happened after that is hazy. But the police wanted to impound the vehicle. Those representing the owners argued that it was necessary for them to have the vehicle and surely some arrangement could be concluded. They gave the police 40,000 shillings and the lorry was spirited away.

I asked what would happen to the families of the two men who died. Insurance? The welfare of their family? The owner would buy food for the funeral and perhaps some sodas and even beer. Maybe even the coffin. And that is that.

Brutal. Harsh. Reality.

Then I happen to read of the eleven-year-old boy murdered by the fourteen-year-old in England. And then the savage behaviour of the Liverpool supporters – no, not supporters – drunks in the pubs outside and away from the ground, who tried to attack and upturn an ambulance because it contained a United player, Alan Smith. Brutal. Savage. Reality. Can you imagine being one of the ambulance men?

But the good news.

The dining hall. All the girls assembled. Dining hall decorated. Tables with new tablecloths, looking splendid. First and second sitting each with new plates. Each child has her own. Each girl now has her very own mug for drinking. Also, newly installed plate racks for draining after the girls wash the plates in the newly built sinks. This term, a stress on manners and the policy of 'graciousness'. Wonderful, or, as one girl said, 'beautiful'. All this alongside their new cookers and stoves and decorated kitchen. One of the teachers was heard to say, 'It's like being at a university.'

See; sometimes, as the poem says, some things do go right!

A small reflection. The power has been off for seven days. The water for four. There are reasons – well, no, not REASONS – for this plight, which deserve a chapter on their own, but it does teach you economy of resources. It is amazing how little water, fetched from the bore hole, you need to bathe in! A full bath; a small basin with a little water, and you can have the whole caboodle (and, of course, the water saved for the cistern!). It just gives you a ridiculous sense of achievement. Ah, but when the water is restored! The luxury, the LUXURY, of a flushing loo.

I'm beginning to worry about myself.

10.03.2006 Poor Little B—s

How can you try to convey the joys and lows of a single day? All crammed into one day. I know I've just written, but listen to this. First, a horror story.

A guy in the village, called Talwana, lives locally in Kibutu, or in a small, small village in Kibutu. To say he was a sandwich short of a picnic would give the wrong impression, because what he said in his incessant chatter was absolutely true, but sometimes inappropriate. He lacked the danger signal the rest of us have, telling us when to speak and when to keep quiet. Therefore, for example, last year he was taken to the police cells and roughed up because he was telling everyone they were corrupt (they are, but you can't blame them), and then showed everyone his bruises.

He was again ill-served during the elections, because he told all and sundry what everyone knew: that the government was corrupt, their chosen candidate the same and people should vote for the sitting MP 'cause she was honest. Not a wise thing to do. One night, they came and strangled him, then stuck him up a tree. The villagers missed him, but it wasn't till his mother reported a strange decaying smell from this tree that they discovered him.

Now, the villagers know who did it (if not the precise men), and the police know who did it, and the message was loud and clear. But even if the police were interested in finding out, they would not have a chance.

Elections free and fair.

Ah, but culture. On the same day as the horror story, or the day I learnt of the horror story, the delights of the classroom.

We have a new first year, and sometimes you forget that some of these girls come from remote villages. So I take them to the library. We look at all the books, and they are to choose a novel a week and read it and write a short review of it. We read together a splendid African short story, and then we discuss it. Then, this week, our first review. I am excited. I write on the board:

- Author
- Characters
- Plot
- What I liked about the book etc.

Pause. Silence. Hand goes up. 'What is an author?'

Ah. Well, she or he is the one who wrote the book. I then go round all the girls to show them who the author is.

Pause. 'What is a character?'

Well… I know. Who likes films? Yes, Nigerian films (God, they're the pits!). Great, tell me your favourite one. All right, the last one. Great, it was a comedy. Who was it about? Yes. Well, he's the main character. Was his friend in it? Well, he's a character. Was his boss in it? Yeah. Well, he's a character. Anyone who is in the story is a character, and the ones who play a big part are the MAIN characters.

Little one (me warming to the idea), what is your favourite film of all time? Pause. Shy smile and a whispered, 'I've never seen a film…' leaves you dumbstruck.

'Well, don't worry, sweetheart, here you'll see lots of films and read lots of books.' (They use my DVD player to watch movies on Saturday afternoons.)

The same day, I teach senior six A level… *King Lear*. Who in their right mind picks bloody Shakespeare for these kids? Yes, yes, I love Shakespeare, but c'mon. And trying to explain the jokes. So they think I am mad. If you have been taught to shut up and take dictation all your life, it is difficult to become active or proactive. Getting them standing in corners, shouting out scenes in their own words is quite daunting. Try it yourself. But we'll get there. We have discovered that, if Lear had had one son instead of or as well as three daughters, he would have saved us all a lot of trouble!

But come, blow winds and crack your cheeks.

They are, however, a delight, and we shall crack the play together!

Bloody water's gone again!

16.03.2006 The Tank

Given the current state of affairs, I would not blame you if you had images of a full-blooded Sherman breaching the gates, trampling over the compound, all machine guns blazing, and in the turret a maniacal soldier shouting out fearsome and loathsome obscenities at all and sundry whilst his big gun fires hell and destruction. Yeah. Here comes Clint Eastwood to the rescue... No, no, no. Calm yourselves. It is not that sort of tank.

That is a tank of war. Ours is a tank of peace and plenitude and blessing and life, not death. Not a tank of war, but a tank of water. 10,000 litres, to be exact. The plumber is fixing it in this week and what a difference it will make. When the electricity goes, it is followed after by the water going. The girls have to resort to local bore holes, and, since the girls are not local, the water can cause some unpleasant reactions in their skin etc. and even sickness. Now, with this new acquisition (courtesy of my generous friends' donations, I might add), water will be treated and safe and ENOUGH! Wow. Besides which, it will save that awful drudge of having to lug these huge heavy gerry cans around. Ain't life grand?

À propos of nothing, but sometimes the girls can capture a picture of what life is for them better than any from the outside; a sudden insight expressed in their own words. I sometimes worry that I can give a distorted picture of life here at school. It is grand. The girls are lovely and forever cheerful and full of fun. The sun, as I am sure I said at some time, does not reveal but hides the reality, because everything is bathed in sunshine and looks lovely. But you are constantly reminded that for the majority life is a struggle; an uphill, relentless (and that is the telling word: relentless) battle. We are constantly being asked for help, for sponsorship, and you do not become hardened to it, but you do what you can and realise you cannot help everyone. Then you get a letter that somehow captures the deep, aching void of poverty. I am relaying this, not because I am seeking or soliciting funds – I am not – but to give you a flavour, a small hint of someone's young life.

An extract:

> First and foremost, I lost both my mother and father in 1995 (when she was eight), and immediately after their death, most of the relatives grabbed the lates' property, rejected us and we were left homeless and desperate. It's only our aunt who took care of us, but unfortunately she died in 2002. This was the most difficult moment I ever had in my life. Our relatives claimed to have so many dependents that they couldn't educate us and accommodate us as well.
>
> However, it is my grandfather who took care of me and my other two sisters; he accepted us, miserable and poor as we were, and we have been living with him up to now. The difficulty is that he is a retired civil servant and is taking care of so many people, other orphaned children, widows, among others.

I think the phrase 'this was the most difficult moment in my life' is heart-stopping. Its simplicity, its starkness, is what is so moving about it. You expect a sentence like that to come out of the mouth of an experienced adult, not someone barely leaving childhood.

Here we are bathed in sunshine. The compound is beautiful. The jacaranda trees, the wonder of the frangipani and the flame trees. A beautiful, beautiful landscape. But her inner landscape must have been as bleak and cold and comfortless as any Dickensian picture.

As I say, *à propos* of nothing, but it was on my mind and I thought I'd share it.

Shopping

Those who know me will rejoice in the fact that today I am off to Kampala to shop. Yes, shop. I have been known to swim the Channel, climb Everest and even watch Liverpool play rather than shop! But today I am shopping for cookers and beds and wardrobes and settees and pots and pans for our new Home Economics Department. Wow. The grant is through and I have the cheque. Ah, sweet mystery of life.

Tonight, I mix with the elite at the British High Commission, at a small gathering for 'small grant' receivers. It may be small to them, but wow! Of course, there'll be snacks and lots of wine; lots of wine… and it's bloody Lent.

Who says God hasn't got a sense of humour!

30.03.2006 None So Blind

I am locked in mortal combat – well, combat – with an eminent UK MP, who was one of the chief observers in the recent elections. That we disagree about the conduct of those elections, I can see, may have been predictable, but what I cannot fathom, condone or understand is his sheer obduracy, his complete denial of what is taking place in Uganda.

I was, am, concerned to the point of obsession by what is going on in the so-called IDP camps. When I pointed out the fact that up to 1,000 people a week were dying in these camps, he flatly refused to believe me or accept the figures. I also referred to the Sydney Peace Talk, in which a renowned Ugandan writer referred to the conflict and situation as 'genocide'. Again, I was told that 'genocide' was not a word to be used lightly.

What annoys me is the implication that I have invented the facts or made up the story of the Peace Talk. I have since sent him the details. In August 2005, the IRIN, a UN organization, in partnership with the Ugandan Ministry of Health, published the findings, the astonishing findings, of 1,000 deaths a week in the camps. The writer/commentator who gave the talk is one Olara Otunnu, a former representative of the UN. He, as would any responsible commentator preparing a brief, prepared it well. He gave the definition of 'genocide' as given by the UN charter and painstakingly illustrated how the events unfolding in the north met all the criteria. Genocide does not necessarily need trains and gas chambers, or people hustled into buildings and burnt alive, or herded into fields and shot *en masse*. There are other means, more subtle, less obvious, but just as effective. Rather like the genocide perpetrated by the whites on the American Red Indians, you drive them from their land, you herd them into concentration camps for twenty years, you slowly strangle their customs and way of life, you make sure there is not enough food and sanitation, and so, slowly, the people die out; die from disease, despair. Malaria,

AIDS, measles, infections, alcohol, whatever. And this is not an oversight, a mistake, a misunderstanding, but a policy based on profit and revenge. Sounds like genocide to me.

Oh, there is also some scam that involves the president's brother and the misappropriation of the former owners' land, but I am still waiting for that report. Meanwhile, if anyone wants to read of the 'protective' activities of the Ugandan army in this region, read the report given out by the Human Rights Watch on the UPDF. Interesting reading of rape, torture, murder, robbery, all done with (I quote) 'impunity'.

Lastly, this MP claimed not I nor anyone else had any evidence of wrongdoing in the election; only hearsay and rumour. Which is why I, as the only one who could use a computer that day (my old friends should read that sentence twice – me, computer), wrote out fourteen affidavits for incredibly brave people in our local constituency claiming harassment and beatings. What they'll get for their trouble, God only knows.

As a Kampala journalist, who directed me to the official sources with the information, said, 'It is amazing how ignorant people in the West are as to what is going on.' Yes, but not if you are an MP with 'expert' knowledge of the country!

30.03.2006 I Love Lucy

I love Lucy. Everybody loves Lucy. Everybody. She is just extraordinary.

What I am now going to outline, you will not understand. I do not understand. It is beyond my experience; outside my rational take on reality; belongs to another dimension, category. I cannot 'get', grasp or understand the mechanics or the economy of 'possession'. We are dealing with a case here at the moment which belongs to deep African culture. Now, let us be careful in our assumptions and judgment. My African friends tell me that, in pre-Christian times, the people – in Uganda, anyway – had a very moral communal religion. It was 'community'-based. They believed in one God, they worshipped together, and, if there was a famine or drought, then, as in biblical times, they offered a sacrifice. There was a strict moral code, and, if you broke it, you harmed the community and were punished by the community. And they did have 'healers' with knowledge, to whom the villagers had recourse in times of sickness and trouble. Only with the introduction of greed and power did this way of life become corrupt, did the healers become witch doctors and the leaders demand sacrifice for themselves so as to claim the carcass of the beast slain. I am not sure when this Garden of Eden was spoilt, but, for time beyond measure, summoning ancestors from the spirit world has been common, and pacts with the devil a form of protection. Even for Christians, it is a sort of hangover, a double insurance, more protection.

Our little girl, or, I should say, tall, elegant girl, was vulnerable right from the beginning. Her father had heaven knows how many women, and her mother wanted to leave the compound without any remembrance or anything belonging to him, so she tried to abort the child. This, for some reason, makes the child open to the powers of evil (because an evil act has been attempted?). This was compounded by the fact that her father at the family home, at great cost, sacrificed a cow, a goat and a hen to Satan and her ancestors, and gave her to him for protection. On hearing this, her mother went to a witch doctor and, in a bowl containing a snake and a head of a sheep, offered sacrifice, then buried the contents on the witch doctor's instructions. Then, her grandfather made some other pact or covenant with the spirits on her behalf.

These are old African village habits, which the Church and other members of society are trying to eradicate. Again, it seems to me the root cause is poverty: people seeking any help to get through life without disaster.

The priest, the wise old priest and his lovely helper, a young married woman with the gift of discernment, are taking this girl into their care. It will involve returning to her village home, persuading her father to break the covenant and repent, then seeking the mother and asking her to break that pact, because, until then, Satan claims her for his own; she has been 'given'. It is urgent, otherwise the girl will 'go mad', they say.

I tell you this not to raise your eyebrows or to make you say 'thank God I live in a civilised world', but to show that this world exists and these sometimes are the forces people have to deal with.

What has this to do with Lucy? She is a light. When the girl was struggling with whatever was disturbing her and, in her delirium, eating ravenously, drinking beaker after beaker of juice and water, the girls would say, 'It's not her, sir, it's the demons.' We stayed until she settled down. Who slept with her that night in the sick bay? Lucy. Who looked after her until the priest arrived the next day? Lucy. When girls become disturbed, or are sick, or are lonely and frightened, who looks after them? Lucy.

If you read the essays written by the newcomers, the first years or girls who enter later, and they recount their first period at the school, Lucy is constantly mentioned as the one who showed kindness and welcome.

The best tribute came at the beginning of term. Parents arrived from Lucy's town, neighbourhood. They wanted their child to come to St Clare's. Oh, good. Why? Because they wanted their daughter to turn out like Lucy. They weren't sure what we did, but whatever it was, they wanted it for their daughter.

I said at the beginning that I do not understand the economy or mechanics of evil and spirits. I don't. And I don't understand the mechanics or economy of it either, but I recognise and rejoice in sheer goodness. Mature, unselfconscious, not the least bit prissy; just kind and caring. I love Lucy.

There are other girls I love and could weep for. There is Dinah (pronounced to rhyme with 'dinner'). She was identified as someone who needed sponsoring. Her father (I think her mother is dead) is a poor, poor villager who is now old and beyond work. The girls here are sometimes still regarded as chattel, property. Last year, when she was twelve years old, her father wanted to sell her into marriage; he would get a good dowry. And to her distress, he did. However, she was rescued by a maternal uncle, another poor villager, just as old, who was struggling with the fees, desperate, but determined to try to save the girl. When he came to the school and was told she was to be sponsored, he was so overcome, so shocked and relieved beyond his hopes, that the poor guy could not speak, could not move. Oh, how I wished his, her sponsors could have seen his face, his reaction; that would have been repayment beyond price.

12.06.2006   Enraptured and Enraged

Enraptured

Liturgy. Liturgy with a smile. No, a grin. Liturgy with exuberance, verve, life, almost ecstasy! The small nearby primary school led the liturgy, and three young male teachers, one playing a sort of small three-stringed harp, led the children in song. Oh, what music, what energy and fun. The young men grinning at each other in the sheer joy and exultation of the children's voices and singing. It was a delight. Think of David in the Old Testament, dancing before the Lord. It was infectious and such a celebration. I wish everyone could hear it, participate in it. And the young children conducting; conducting with their arms, their shoulders, their elbows, their eyes. Ah! As my grandson would say, 'It rocks.'

Such is the community, the church at its best. It was so good.

Enraged

A small band of between fifty and seventy children come every night to say the rosary at our house. They are faithful and devout. They say the rosary and end up singing, singing hymns in English or their mother tongue. It is not the exuberant, full metal blast of the full church singing, but softer, gentler and so harmonious. I joke not when I say it is harmonious, celestial, innocent.

Then, one night, after the rosary, one lovely girl came to say she was forbidden to use the little rosary we gave her, because a priest had had a vision, and in this vision Our Lady was weeping tears of blood because the flag of victory on that cross was in fact a snake of Satan. She may have been weeping blood; I was spitting blood. There is a lot of Satanism and devil worship in the country, but this was plain wicked. A priest friend who deals a lot with Satanism said not only that it was ridiculous but that it would mean Christ was defeated.

How can anyone turn what is a holy prayer, a sacred and innocent enterprise, into a thing of evil? Saw visions. It's a pity they can't see the evil in front of their noses, instead of frightening old ladies and children with their superstitious rubbish. Why don't they fight the corruption in their own country and government? Why don't they question that 400 people die EVERY WEEK, and mostly children, because they have no access to drugs, because they've been filched by everyone along the line? Why don't they challenge a country that allows its top ministers to rob the Global Fund of millions and millions of dollars to line their own pockets? Or the schools, primary, which have 150–200 children per class and call it 'universal education' and then pay the teachers a pittance WHEN they pay them? Or the dirty, overcrowded hospitals? Or the harassed staff? Or the wonderful hierarchy (with the exception of the bishop of Gulu) who never take to task the government's criminal neglect of the Acholi tribe and the thousands in the displaced camps? That's Satan at work, not the beads of innocent children.

Yep. Not impressed.

21.06.2006 Gulu: Conflicting Emotions

The Journey
It had taken a long time to arrange; far longer than I anticipated, but at last it was arranged. I had originally tried to go through a brilliant young man called Stephen Okello, who works for Uganda Conflict Action Network, who can quote from the UN Human Rights Charter at will (and, as far as I know, every other charter as well), and who is so versed in the history and politics and twists and turns of the conflict that he may be counted as a real expert. Unfortunately, all the contacts he gave me were either unavailable or just weren't answering.

I tried to go through a priest friend with whom I was in a workshop in Gulu two years ago. Again, he was unavailable and, guessing by the number of calls I made over several weeks, may well be out of the country.

At last, I was given the number of the chairman of the local council, a powerful figure who gave up being an MP so as to serve locally. Over the phone, he was warm, enthusiastic and very inviting, and we arranged to meet on Friday 16 June in his office in Gulu.

Because it is safer to travel via Kampala, I went on Thursday. I had a wretched night staying at a guest house, with the double whammy of being eaten alive by God knows what insects and being treated throughout the night to a canine chorus with barking, wailing and howling. Lovely.

The next morning, it took us an hour to get through Kampala (I hired David, the usual driver. I don't drive to or through Kampala; it's the survival instinct!).

The journey was long and tiring but good. Once again, I marvelled at the beauty and greenery of Uganda. Talk about forty shades of green, and the bright yellow and purple and red flowers in the trees and bushes; profuse. And fields and fields of sunflowers and rich fertile land. However, two things happened on the way, which saddened and sickened me somewhat.

We passed through a so-called town (big trading centre), and there was some commotion. The crowd was jostling and high-spirited and at first I thought it was a circumcision party, with the same excited noise. Then I saw the young man who was tied to a rope, arms bound, being hurried along by the crowd. He looked young and strong and angry and definitely defiant. The mob was mainly young men, who were very high but cheerful and in an almost carnival atmosphere. As they ran, he turned one way and another, trying to see where the next light assault would come from. David said, thief. They would give him a severe beating and then give him to the police, he thought. The young man was lucky; often, they are killed or burned alive, as happened in Mbale last week. The mob looked happy, but you can never judge the mood and volatility of a mob.

David said he was a thief; probably stole a chicken or 1,000 shillings (30p) and perhaps stole it for his family. David said we catch and punish or kill the poor thieves. The rich ones (government ministers) we let get away.

Then he launched into a story about the poverty in Mbale, where we had travelled from and where he lives. Last week, a friend and fellow private taxi man, the same age as David, twenty-eight, was hired to go the Kenyan border. He did not know it was a smuggling operation. When they went to get the parcels (contraband cigarettes), the police were ready. David's friend was shot dead; the smuggler got away. Poverty.

Gulu

We arrived in Gulu. I made my way to the LC's office. The LC rejoices in the unlikely and wonderful name of Norbert Mao. No, he'd gone to Hotel Pearl Afrique. Go there.

No, he's in a meeting. Please stay in the reception area.

One hour later. I'll be in the bar.

One hour later; he has just had to walk out with someone. Please wait.

One hour later. Mr Mao? Oh, he's gone. He won't be back.

I lost it. It had taken a great deal of time, a considerable amount of money and a great deal of effort. And then this! My outburst produced the same puzzled expression that they always give if you raise your voice, like 'what is the matter with this guy?'

Eventually, Mao's deputy came and said he did not know of my coming. We then had a conversation about why I was there (solidarity, to bear witness, to hear what the people in the camp had to say or to relate). We arranged to meet the next day, when he would take me to one of the camps. Then I returned to stay in the guest house of St Mary's hospital in Lacor. I shall return to the hospital later.

The Camp

It takes between twenty and thirty minutes to reach the camp. A little of the background.

When the LRA began its atrocious and terrifying abductions and killings and mutilations, the army and the government suspected that it had either active collaborators or silent covert sympathisers amongst the Acholi people. Of course, the majority, the vast majority, were not. A radical and desperate solution was resolved upon: within twenty-four hours, people were turned off their land and herded into areas that were to become camps. There weren't camps there as such; they had to build their own. It was claimed it was for their 'protection' (a new and novel way to use the word) and they were forced to go on pain of death. Twenty-four hours. You can imagine how much logistical and strategic planning went into that. Of course, the camps offered no such protection, and the crimes committed by the UPDF are too numerous to recount: rape, torture, drownings, murder. An army more of occupation than liberation. Thus the camps.

I went to visit Camp Paicho. I was amazed, moved and totally surprised. It completely confounded my expectations.

The camp is comprised of hundreds of African conical mud and grass huts. And what strikes you immediately is how clean it is. They sweep the compound thoroughly every day. Everything was orderly, neat, well kept. I then formally met five young men in one of the buildings, smartly dressed in shirts and trousers, who carried themselves with authority and presence. One, Vincent, was the camp 'commander'; the others were subcommanders. We spoke through an interpreter, although they all spoke very good English, except Vincent. I asked Vincent how many were in the camp, and he replied, without hesitation, '17,318.' He knew the exact number.

I asked, if they were in the House of Commons or could speak to the MPs, what would they say? What would be their concerns and plea?

Vincent said they had three main concerns:

Health. Many were dying; about fifteen a week in his camp. The medical staff who were supposed to come did not, or, if they did, they did not stay. The sanitation is poor and water is difficult to get from the bore holes. There are no drugs.

Education. So many children, no education.

Food. Since the beginning of the year, the World Food Programme has cut back on the supply of food.

The other upright, stalwart young men then spoke in turn. Frederick wanted an end to the war through peace talks and amnesty. The others unanimously and enthusiastically agreed. No court; reconciliation (I believe that Kony and others should be brought to justice, but have I the right to hold such views?).

The others said pressure must be put on both sides, especially the government, to pursue peace and not break off talks as in the past.

The UK should broker the peace talks; put pressure on the government and the LRA, as the international community had done in Darfur.

The government doesn't have the political will to end the war; it should be made to do so.

They do not think the war will end.

All they want is peace, peace, peace, peace, peace.

I was then shown round the campsite. As I said, it was impressively clean and smart. Wherever we went, we were pursued by a posse of laughing, giggling children astounded to see a white man. They would gleefully shout out '*mono*' (I think), meaning 'white man'. Yes, they really do exist.

When a member dies, they are buried immediately outside their hut. The camp is littered with graves, everywhere you go; sadly, most of them are tiny: the graves of children. We passed an aged granny with an ageless face, on whose lap her four-year-old granddaughter laid her head. She had yellow fever. The beautiful little one saw the white man, and she did not have the strength to raise her head, but she did raise a beautiful smile.

We saw the children pump the water from the bore hole; very hard work. I was told it was in their culture that women and children bore the responsibility for fetching water. Have you ever carried a gerry can of water? Do you know how heavy it is? I'm afraid I internally bristled at that, but it was the only time.

Before we leave the camp, I must mention what an acute sense of humour these young men had. When going round, I asked how people became camp commanders or zone leaders (the camp is divided into zones, each with its own leader, and each site has a clearing where the people meet and discuss). By election. How often? Every four years. Pause. Smile. Are they allowed to stand for a third term? Hilarity. They broke out into huge gleeful laughter and much slapping of hands. Their laughter is uninhibited, delighted, spontaneous, like children. They love weak jokes, and so I love them. At the end of the visit, I asked the ever-alert and charming Frederick which football team he supported (but God knows when or how they could see a football match). There was a pause. Ever-polite hosts. England. No, which premiership team? Arsenal. WHAT? If I'd known that, he would not have been allowed into the meeting. Well, it was the best joke in the world! Leaping with laughter; what football team did I support? Leaping even farther. Arms raised. Man U. That caused even more delight.

Finally, before going, the youngest guy said, 'I want to say something for the young people. We need training. We need to be "constructionalists"; builders, brick layers, carpenters. We need to learn. We need to earn.'

I left the camp, deeply impressed and deeply moved.

The night before, I had stayed in a guest house in St Mary's Lacor. A wonderful, beautiful hospital; clean, sparkling, hygienic, with medical wards, surgical wards, an intensive care unit, a nutrition unit, paediatric ward; a hospital with plenty of well-trained staff and nurses. But even in this well-guarded compound, the old mind was on alert; not red alert, but conscious that this was a war zone. What about those in the camps, with no walls, no guards, no protection? How do you cope?

Commuters

The saddest sight of all was the sight of hundreds of little and teenage children pouring into a section of the hospital to sleep; the commuters. They do this every day and every night; no weekends off. Most of the parents stay behind. These kids are rootless. They are unruly and will probably grow up to be unlawful, ungovernable. They have no culture and have lost, or, rather, never been given the African way. They have no respect for their elders or, indeed, for anyone. They pour in to find shelter and safety. They do not always succeed. Some girls have to pay for shelter with sex, which gives a whole new twisted meaning to 'safe sex'. Some of the boys become petty thieves. They are worse off than children in the camps, because there you get a sense of community, a sense of a cohesive unified society, of belonging. These kids, on the other hand, are, in many ways, abandoned, betrayed.

The Future

We need, as NGOs, as international agencies, to pour massive resources into these regions, to heal and to give a future to these people. We need to alert the world. We need a 'Studs Terkel' type of oral history, so that the people can tell their own story. We need to train the young men and women in every sort of skill, and especially to teach the skill of making solar stoves to stop the reliance on firewood, which is now a scarce resource (Sr Cosmas's idea; brilliant).

We need, above all, to stop the war. I do not believe it is beyond our wit or means.

Gulu. It was a long journey. It was an even longer emotional one.

26.06.2006 Oops!

Keeping your finger on the pulse. Or things not to be discussed in polite society.

Now, ladies, this is not for you. We all know that ladies do not have the same biological eruptions or indeed functions or malpractices of their male counterparts. They do not express wind forcefully from any orifice; they do not even ever so slightly burp (is there a more onomatopoeic word than 'burp'? You can whisper it; prolong it: 'burrrrp'; shorten it: 'brp'; declaim it: 'BURP'; wonderful word). Anyway, getting back to the subject in hand (or should that be finger?): ladies live, thank God, away from all such crudities. So, ladies, avert your eyes.

There is raging in the papers here an argument about driving and the use of one's hands. In the UK, it's about driving and the illegal use of the mobile phone. 'Cause here, they are wondering whether to make 'digital nasal excavation' a motoring offence. Yep. Here, digital nasal excavation is more than a pastime; it is a national sport, a hugely popular and enduring occupation and preoccupation. No fastidiousness here, mate; get right on at it!

Everyone, EVERYONE, does it, with the lack of self-consciousness that a bird has when taking to flight. In class, at the bus stop, in the taxi, in staff meetings, anywhere! And not only the nasal excavation. The ear excavation. But that is not confined to the digital experience. You are talking to someone in an office and you see a pencil disappearing down someone's lughole; a few twists and turns and out it comes, without a shadow of emotion or embarrassment on the said person's face. And, if you are talking of *King Lear* to an enthusiastic but barely comprehending little group, 'disconcerting' is the word as you see a finger fast disappearing up the left nostril, the student all the time looking at you as if nothing is happening. Do you say 'What on Earth are you doing?' or 'Put that away' or 'Not here, not now, dear' or what? And it is to my astonishment that they never seem to notice the open-mouthed startled expression on my face! And why is it that when they have extracted, they examine their retrieved treasure with such admiration?

But that is culture. To them, it is a sheer bliss, a harmless and free expression of indulging in something that gives them pleasure and release; not for them the closed toilet door and the grabbing of tissue paper and job done and thoroughly washed hands. Nope. Go for it. Enjoy it. Vigour. Enthusiasm. Unimpeded, uninhibited joyous fun.

I do not know about the rest of Africa, but if it ever becomes an Olympic sport, my money's on Uganda for gold.

Well, ladies, you can now open your eyes and continue with what you were doing.

14.07.2006 *In Praise of Youth*

If only I were twenty! I am now living with three young girls. Honest. Two belong to an organisation that sends out kids for a year before they start university, and one is a postgrad. over here for two months. How they all ended up here is a strange and wondrous story; suffice to say they needed rescuing. So, this young, energetic, enthusiastic, whirlwind bunch of girls... it's killing me. I'd forgotten how much young people eat! And, having lived in splendid isolation for a couple of months, it's disconcerting to bump into a bra in the bathroom (unoccupied bra, I hasten to add). But they are a breath of fresh air and are wonderful.

They are working up in the Leonard Cheshire Rehabilitation Home just up the road and doing great work. One is only here for five weeks, the American girl, and the other two (one Irish and one half-Portuguese half-Welsh) for three months. They get on as though they have known each other all their lives.

In working at the home, they have found it rewarding and heartbreaking. These kids range in age from seven to late teens. They suffer from such disabilities as polio, osteomyelitis, club foot and even deformed feet and hands. Most are on crutches, some in wheelchairs. So the first thing we decided in council round the kitchen table was to interview all the kids and all the staff individually. We devised a questionnaire that got the kids to talk about themselves, their abilities, how they saw themselves, their future, their ambitions, their earliest memories, who they trusted, and with whom could they share their feelings, what they thought of the home and what they would like to see happen. The girls split up and carried out the interviews over the next few days.

Wow. What a revelation. I think it may have been the first time they were given an opportunity to talk about themselves, and, of course, it was heartbreaking. To get a grasp of it, you have to understand how the Africans, especially the village Africans, can look on the disabled. Very often, they are rejected because they are a bad omen, bringing bad luck or evidence of a curse, a sign that the ancestral spirits are angry etc. Some are even abandoned or starved. Some developed their disability later on in life, as with polio, and recall how their father used to love them. One beautiful, brave lady, when her son was rejected, left her husband and now lives with her son. Many are marginalised and are not accepted.

Their ambitions? Mainly to be able to help other people. They are happy when they are with their friends and when they can help people, and as one said when being interviewed, 'right now'. They are incredible and beautiful. Sadly, they also uncovered a case of physical and psychological abuse, which is being dealt with!

Meanwhile, the girls are working wonders. They have dug a huge garden (roping in another male volunteer to help them dig), are building a chicken house and have opened a small library, made all sorts of educational toys and posters (the house has been turned into a workshop!) and generally galvanised the whole place. Wow!

We've had endless trouble with power going off, water shortages etc., but they bear it all with great good humour and zest.

They are great... but I think I now need a quiet room and a rest!

Oh, names: Catrina (Cat), Jessie and Amber.

15.07.2006 End of Project Report

It is time to look back on the last two years and give a brief account of the stage of the journey we have now reached. A lot of changes have taken place, and it is important that we set these down on paper so as to reflect and evaluate. There have been changes in personnel, in procedures, and there have been significant changes in the physical appearance of the school.

Physical Changes
These changes are important because they reflect the importance we attach to the environment as a means of instilling in the girls a sense of their own inherent worth. If the girls abide in an aesthetically pleasing environment, with obvious care and attention placed on it, it has a profound effect on their appreciation of their surroundings and the value they place upon themselves.

1   MANHOLES COVERED
There used to be a strong smell emitting from these broken manholes, which did nothing to create a sense of belonging or care. It is in attention to such detail that the right atmosphere and ethos is created. That, and the large gaping hole or well had to be fixed so as not to be a danger to anyone on the campus.

The headteacher and the principal initiated a termly physical audit of the school, and these resulted in drawing attention to the maintenance programme. The first audit, for example, revealed over twenty windows that needed replacing and many tubes that were useless or broken. This was obviously unsatisfactory, and as a result we now make sure the windows are examined weekly, as are the tubes, and replaced immediately.

The classrooms, hall etc. are regularly redecorated.

2   DINING HALL
The dining hall has been transformed, as has the way in which the

students attend their meals. We have allotted specific places to all students, each table having its own plates, and the plates are washed and put into draining lockers. Each table also has a tablecloth and a cloth with which to wipe the table. When the table leaders have set out the food, the students say grace before eating.

3 KITCHEN

The kitchen has also been transformed, newly decorated, with new stainless steel stoves, and all that it needs now is a small outbuilding in which to house the wood. We have also built new outdoor sinks in which the students wash their plates.

4 LIBRARY

The library has been physically moved from a dark, uninviting classroom to its present light location. The books originally in the library were, for all intents and purposes, useless and had to be given to infant schools. An enormous amount of new stock was bought, and now each department has a set of textbooks and each student has at her disposal the opportunity to read a novel a week.

We also purchased new tables and mats, and the students use the library frequently and are very happy to study in it. We have also erected new display boards in the library and hired a librarian.

5 TEACHERS' STAFF ROOM

The teachers' staff room badly needed attention, with no furniture, not even chairs. The teachers now have two large tables around which they can meet (staff meetings etc., a big impact on how meetings are conducted), chairs, beautifully-made lockers and a TELEVISION (World Cup!). It shows far more appreciation of the staff and how they are valued.

6 COMPUTER SUITE

Another innovation that has reaped benefits has been the purchasing of computers, the training of staff, the setting up of the computer suite and being linked to the Internet. Naturally, the students have responded enthusiastically. We are, at the moment, applying for another forty computers, which we hope to get next year.

7 NETS

Finally, in the continued effort to raise the self-esteem and health of the girls, we got a new mosquito net for each student and, indeed, teacher. They are excellent nets and should have a significant impact on the cases of malaria with which we are plagued in this part of Uganda.

Systems

The hub and heart of every school is its staff and staff dynamics: how they see themselves; how they see the school; whether they feel part of it; whether they 'own' it or whether they feel unimportant and irrelevant. The first task we undertook was eliciting from the staff their own hopes and wishes and ambitions. We (the headteacher and principal) carried out lengthy interviews with each member of staff, which were recorded and then typed up and given back to each member. It was, in fact, the beginning or first step of appraisal.

Next, we started the weekly staff meetings. We had a long meeting in which we asked each member of the staff what changes they would make in the school if they had a wish. Anne (God bless her) took a note of everyone's contribution. We then typed those up and reported back to the staff. The chief concern was the lack of security in their jobs, and they greatly desired contracts. The directors readily agreed and we won them two-year contracts. A year later, we had another staff meeting and went through their 'wish' list, and everything they desired had come about.

1 OTHER SYSTEMS

In order to develop good practice, we introduced a whole range of new initiatives. There is the weekly staff meeting, which is really a briefing but can lead to longer staff meetings.

There are now lesson observations (which they see as helpful and supportive). There are yearly appraisals, weekly religious assemblies, monthly Masses, the setting up of clubs, the establishment of a prefect body, the visiting of other schools, professional development and, very importantly, the School Development Plan, in which all are involved.

Perhaps the most important initiative, however, is the

monthly meeting with the director, which has an agenda and is minuted. This gives a sense of direction, a sense of mutual support, and gives all parties an opportunity to reflect and discuss.

2   VOCATIONAL STUDIES

The most exciting development has been the launch into vocational studies; this opens up a whole new world for the school. It must be remembered that the school is really still in its infancy. The directors have purchased sixteen acres of land; these will be worked by the students, who will grow crops and develop skills in animal husbandry. This land will not only feed the school and give them a healthier diet, but, if the chicken run succeeds, will generate income that can be used to offset part of the fees for the poorer students.

3   HOME ECONOMICS

We have set up the Home Economics department with its cooking facilities and its 'home': a large kitchen for several pupils at a time to develop their cooking skills, front room, bedroom, toilet and bathroom, sewing and tailoring room etc. The pupils may well begin to have other courses, such as health and beauty, as well as catering. The idea is to enable the students to be job creators, or at least be skilled enough to till their own gardens and plots efficiently and live off the land. There are exciting times ahead, and great opportunities.

Assets

The school has many assets, not least of which is a dedicated director with drive and ambition for the school. It also has a very wise and dedicated headteacher, and, in the main, a very committed staff with talent and initiative. With that talent and goodwill, the school should thrive.

1   THE STUDENTS

How could you end a report without mentioning the greatest asset the school possesses: its girls? They are so hard-working, so cheerful, so uncomplaining and such a delight to be with. They sing like angels and extract the greatest fun and glee from the simplest things. High-spirited, grateful, funny and lovely. It has been a wonderful privilege to have a great many of them sponsored by my incredibly generous friends and family back home. And, of course, most of the changes we made could not have happened without my family and friends. I wish I could convey to them the impact their generosity has had on the girls' lives. The girls will never forget them, and neither shall I.

26.07.2006 Wheels within Wheels

I am not sure how much notice is being taken of the political scene here, but we are set for some profound change in the near future. The war with Phony Kony may be near its end, but not to everyone's satisfaction.

Kony is leader of the so-called Lord's Resistance Army, which, for twenty years, has prosecuted the most barbaric and cruel war against the local population in the regions of Gulu, southern Sudan and the Congo. His weapons have been abducting, maiming, killing and generally terrorising the civilian population. His abduction of children into his army has been particularly harrowing, often forcing them to butcher their own fathers and mothers or siblings by hacking them to death. The people, especially the Acholi, have suffered immensely.

They have, however, suffered not only at the hands of the LRA, but also at the hands of the UPDF, the Ugandan army that was meant to protect them. In order to avoid even tacit support that might be given to these rebels, one and a half million people were forced from their homes into IDP camps (some say concentration camps), where they have languished for twenty years. They estimate a thousand people a week die in these camps, not violently (that figure is only 146) but from alcohol, TB, malaria and AIDS. Some say that, in Museveni's eyes, it was nothing less than they deserved for being on the wrong side in the war and that 'they are like grasshoppers in a bottle, killing themselves'.

The story is further complicated by the rapes, murders, intimidation and brutality of the UPDF. Many of the top brass in the army have made enormous sums from this war, and it is in their interests to keep the war going. Since Museveni could not win and did not show much interest in winning this war, he called in the International Criminal Court to bring Kony to justice at The Hague. This is not as simple as it appears. It became apparent that Kony would defend himself and that all the heinous crimes committed by the army would also come out, and Museveni himself would be implicated for compliance in these crimes, or at least neglect.

There are two sides to this vexing question. The Acholi people traditionally favour reconciliation (they have no death penalty) and are anxious to stop the war at any price. They are further confused that the ICC would go after the LRA alone and not the others who commit crimes (UPDF).

Museveni does not want the international community's eyes on him or his army; he knows it would not stand up to scrutiny. To the outrage of the ICC, Museveni is offering Kony and his cronies immunity. A neat trick; he is seen as bringing this dreadful war to an end and avoids censure.

What will the ICC say? What can they say? What will the international community say or do? Sod all, I imagine.

I want the war to end, because the people I talked to in the camps do. But I also want Kony and his gang brought to justice.

26.07.2006 Books, Bricks, Canvas and Porridge

Coming out to the living room at 7.45 a.m., bleary-eyed and not quite conscious, I am met with the vision of my adopted daughters running a workshop/factory. These are the youngsters working at the Rehabilitation Home. They are sandpapering and painting bricks (educational toys) for the little ones at the home, felt-tipping designs for games on sewn-up white canvas bags, making letters and making 'porridge' for papier maché to construct the solar system. A fellow can only take so much.

I live now in a cross between a girls' dormitory and an artists' commune! My life has been taken over. I am not sure whether I am suffering from exhaustion or exhilaration; either way, I'm punch drunk.

How quickly you forget how much energy they have, how huge their appetites, how stark raving mad and giddy they are. Ah, for the solace of a quiet pub! And music! Don't ask.

Still, they have transformed the home. They've started a little library, interviewed each of the disabled children and the staff at length, dug a garden, planted fruit trees and pineapple whatnots, decorated all the halls and dining rooms with letters and maps, made a playground with a swing, and made games for the kids. The kids love them, as do the staff. Last Sunday, they threw the kids a party, and the kids kept wondering who would be coming to visit. They could not believe it was for them. Well, it was, and what a party. Loads of food; fizzy drinks; games, including races on crutches and in wheelchairs, and dancing, dancing, dancing. It was a great party and lasted from 11 a.m. to 5 p.m. Wow.

I really do need to lie down.

The home will never be the same after the hurricane of those three has hit it. The good news is they have replacements coming in September. Great.

02.08.2006 Dreams

Before we begin, let me say I do not understand this story; or, rather, I can't explain it or get my head round it. It is the sort of thing Oscar Wilde (one of my heroes) would write.

Fr Carlos Rodrigues is one of the heroes in Uganda. He is a priest working for many years in the north, serving the Acholi. He has been harassed and arrested and intimidated – well, they tried to intimidate – but he still goes on serving his people. He has been in touch with Kony, with anyone, as he tries to save his people and broker peace.

He tells this story that happened last week. A sort of uneasy peace and security in the north, after many years, has returned; well, a sort of security.

> Eveline is a four-year-old child living in Gulu...
>
> It will always remain deeply engraved in my memory, the image of Eveline's sad eyes looking at me from her mother's lap. I can assure you that few things in life have made me so depressed. The whole family was present when I presided over the burial of four children killed during an all-night rebel attack one day in January 2003. The little girl could not stop crying during the whole funeral service, and neither could I.
>
> As she started taking her first steps and uttering her first words, she found herself joining the legion of about 40,000 kids who those days trekked to town every night looking for a safe place to sleep. Her parents tell me how she used to have nightmares and how worried they were when watching her little body shiver at night.
>
> ...Because of the great improvement in security, she, like many of her small-age mates, doesn't have to walk to town for safety.
>
> Slowly, she is forgetting about her previous nasty dreams, and her body doesn't shake because of fear any more. Some three weeks ago, however, her heart was heavy with sadness, because her mother fell sick with high fever and nothing could make her

recover. One night, she sneaked into her parents' room and woke up Mum. She had just had a dream, she explained with persistent conviction. God had whispered to her to come under the mango tree in the homestead compound as soon as it dawned and there pick a medicinal plant that would cure Mum and make her well. Her parents stared at her, speechless. Once she had finished delivering the important message, Eveline went back to her sleeping mat and closed her eyes for the rest of the night.

As soon as the sky turned red, they rushed to the big tree in the compound. There, they saw a plant, which, as far as they could remember, had not been there the night before. Eve's dad prepared a concoction and gave it to Mum to drink. In the evening, she was able to get up. The following day, she slowly resumed her daily chores. Eveline smiled and told all her classmates about the dream in which God told her how to find the right medicine to heal her mum.

For many years, I have heard plenty of stories in Acholi about people who dream about healing remedies, but it was my first time to see a kid who receives such revelations, and – what can I tell you? – personally, I find it fascinating to live in a place where children who used to have war nightmares talk to God in dreams and can make their mothers have good health.

I write it as I found it. Astounding, touching. Beyond our little reason.

02.08.2006 Incidents

The saddest thing, or the thing that I wish I could change, is the inability to speak or, more importantly, listen to and understand the local language – or, in the case of Uganda, local languages (fifty-six). Like everyone else, the Ugandans comprise of the astute, the dim, the downright clever and bright, the slow-witted, the sharp and cynical, the arrogant, the ignorant, the generous and kind. The banter on the *matatus* (minibuses used as taxis) was very sharp and very funny, and if Betty, the head, had not witnessed it, I would have missed it.

The scene is a woman getting on board the minibus, meant to cater for fourteen but squeezing in up to twenty. If a child sits on her lap, they don't pay for the child's seat. She has two children, one of four and one nearly two. But she hops to the bus because the other leg is lame, and her head drops to one side because of some lameness in her shoulder.

'How much to Mbale?'

'1,000 shillings.'

'I only have 800.'

There is a general movement in the bus as everyone starts to look for the other 200. No one says a word.

One woman says to the lady, 'Who is going to hold your baby?'

'You look as though you are merciful. I thought you would.'

The woman laughs and takes the baby.

Africans, or at least Ugandans, are interested in life, but are especially fascinated with each other. Everyone is now captivated by the woman's spirit and verve.

A man asks, 'Are these your children?' Everyone wanted to ask that question but refrained for fear of giving offence.

'Oh, yes, of course they are my children. I need them for when I get old. They will look after me.' So the conversation goes. Without a trace of self-pity, the woman, who is neatly dressed and whose children, like her, are very smart and cleanly turned out, says, 'I am very strong. I dig in my garden every day.'

They arrive at her destination. The taxi conductor, who belongs to a set of people who would rob the Pope, very sharp and quick to take every advantage, says, 'On you go,' and does not take a shilling for the fare. Off she hops. She leaves behind a quiet admiration and a silver moment of a touch of kindness and compassion; everyone is glad to have encountered her.

And the banter. The taxi drivers were furious that Museveni got re-elected. As I say, they are sharp. They blame the villagers for being fools, and they blame women. So furious were they with the women that there was serious talk about raising the taxi fares for women! That's what you'd call 'positive discrimination', I imagine!

13.08.2006 And Now the End Is Near…

What a day. What a day. Unforgettable. It was, indeed, the long goodbye.

It began with Mass. The priest was a mere one and a half hours late, but this is Africa. While the kids were waiting for him, they sat and sang. I think they sang every known hymn in Christendom and some that are unknown, but they displayed the usual incredible patience and perseverance.

The Mass was lovely and the girls sang like angels.

After Mass, everything was cleared away and the entertainment began. Well, it lasted all day and it was brilliant. The various classes all sang welcome songs, and then they launched into 'traditional' songs and dances. WOW! They were stunning, and some of them SO funny. There were songs and dances about barren women trying to get babies by going to the village witch doctor, songs and dramas about drunken husbands pleading for forgiveness (including Speciosa's drunk, which was the best drunk I've ever seen on stage!) and a host of others. This was followed by a drama. What a drama. An old, cunning chief tried to marry the princess, thereby becoming king, and he had plotted to let the king die (brilliant performances) but was exposed and thereupon killed the princess and committed suicide. By heavens, they love blood and drama. Wonderful. Talk about African magic. It was hilarious; the kids LOVED it, and so did I.

Then the head girl, Lucy, made a speech extolling my virtues; all of it true, of course, but in truth it was so touching and so well written. She reportedly said afterwards that she had been nervous, but it didn't show. She was assured and purposeful and poised. It was wonderful. Others, including the director and head, made very nice little speeches too, but Lucy's, ah, it caught me.

Then we all went to the compound and witnessed my planting the Patrick tree (they call me Patrick here). Two teachers are now vying as to who waters the tree in my absence, and I've told them not to drown it!

Then lunch. Prepared by the girls in our new Home Economics department. Lovely.

Then more entertainment and, as guest of honour, I had to make a little reply speech. Then the presentation of gifts, from the head and the staff and the girls. Speechless.

The evening rounded off with my doing the first dance with Western music (not cowboy music; music from the West). Well, I wasn't going to let the side down. Suffice it to say, I 'shook my ass', and Africans know how to shake ass, and they loved it and I loved it. Halfway through, I got the secretary up to dance; she is BIG, but can she move! Then all the girls joined in. It was magic. It was wonderful.

Then to the staff room and a few beers with, I am sure, the whole school looking in through the windows. Oh, a small detail: I had my photo taken with about 200 individual girls!

It was overwhelming. In my little parting speech, I, of course, thanked several people. All and sundry, staff, director, especially Betty the head, the non-teaching staff, Winnie, groundsmen etc. But most of all I thanked the girls. It has been such a privilege and pleasure sharing their young lives. I told them all the usual things, but I also told them I loved them. And I do. So much.

Now, if you'll excuse me, I am going to a quiet corner… to cry.

13.08.2006 Uganda

It was an open and shut case. Or, at least, it should have been. In a way, it was, except that the case was not so much shut as slammed.

Juliet Kafire Rainer, an opposition MP for many years, was popular, very popular, amongst her constituents. She was not a Cinderella MP, turning up for an hour at the ball, but worked consistently and constantly for the good of her constituents: fighting cartels who tried to keep the price of cotton down; tackling government and local corruption; starting small businesses to find the villagers employment; starting all sorts of community projects. Well-liked; indeed, loved and looked up to by the voters. She approached the election with considerable confidence. But this is Uganda. She lost her seat.

Juliet, however, is a wise old bird. She took note and she collected evidence. She challenged the outcome. I saw and read the dossier she submitted to the court. She had photographic evidence of the unmarked pick-up truck used to ferry the mob of violent supporters of the government's NRM candidate; she had photographs of the chief of police with the sticks used to beat and intimidate the voters; she had seven affidavits from brave constituents who had been badly beaten by these gangs; she even had proof that the candidate was ineligible to stand for Parliament because he was still a serving soldier and had not the required academic qualifications (the documents he had were obviously forged and gave him more academic clout than Einstein, whereas he finished at P7). To top it all, the returning officer gave evidence that he had witnessed the beatings and intimidation and the stuffed ballot boxes with pre-ticked papers.

I said to Madam Rainer that she had a brilliant case. She said, 'You never know with our judiciary.'

The judgment was incredibly swift for Uganda. The result was upheld because the evidence presented did not have any real effect on the election! When I expressed my horror, she simply said, 'Pray for Uganda. Pray for my country.'

I do.

But this is Uganda.

Mao

In the north, we have these protracted peace talks taking place. There is much manoeuvring. I had a furious exchange with Norbert Mao over his hugging Kony in a gesture that I found bewildering. He embraced him like a long-lost brother. I found it nauseating and told Mao so. He was livid. I think that Kony besmirches the name 'Rebel', that he and his lieutenants are not rebels but psychopaths. Mao made two points that I believe are valid. He claimed that, if we were going to seek justice, then all those who have committed heinous crimes, such as rape and torture and murder and intimidation and terror, should be brought to trial, and that the people in the camps could not understand why the UPDF were not indicted as well. He further claimed that his people wanted above all, at any price, peace. This, of course, suits Museveni, whose part in this dreadful and horrible war would be exposed. We parted on friendly terms, even if we disagreed.

I note, by the way, that the US faith leaders, in urging Bush to support the peace talks, reiterate the figure of up to one thousand deaths a week in the camps, first published by the World Health Organisation.

Museveni

Andrew Mwenda, an investigative reporter with *The Daily Monitor*, who was imprisoned last year for criticising the president, is of the opinion that Museveni is the new Mugabe. The one little sign of hope is that the mask is beginning to slip and his mammoth greed is being exposed. The US has become alarmed that the government is now a personalised institution with no checks or balances in place. Five out of seven judges deemed the election unfair but were frightened to overturn the result because they knew Museveni would go to war. The judges were even murmuring their discontent with the 'safe' houses (what an appallingly sickening ironic name: 'safe'), where people disappear and are killed or tortured. But it is the sheer rapaciousness of his open greed that appals. The Ministry of Agriculture, Animal Industry and Fisheries, which contributes 34% of the Gross Domestic Product and employs 73% of Uganda's citizens, gets an annual budget of a mere 9.6 billion shillings, whereas the presidency has a budget of 88 billion! The state is now entirely personalised.

When the UPDF was about to launch Operation Iron Fist, it was discovered that the Fourth Division had 2,400 troops and 4,800 ghost soldiers! The Presidential Guard Brigade boasts over 10,000!

I fear for Uganda. Now that oil has been discovered, there is already an unseemly rush for land grabbing. Who, I wonder, will benefit from this windfall?

There are many problems, with lack of water; rising HIV/AIDS, malaria; poverty; hunger; lack of drugs; above all, corruption at every level. My deep, deep wish and desire is that we in the West do not become complicit in these crimes and that we do not condone or support this growing abuse of power and abuse of the people of Uganda.

23.08.2006 Litany

When I was young, a child, and even beyond childhood, there was a cunning plan devised by some irreligious zealot to turn people off God and anything to do with religion under the guise of prayer. This ploy used the device of a custom called litanies. Litanies (I still hear the monotonous drone) were invented to induce in the poor benighted participant – no, too strong a word – hearer, reciter, whatever, a sort of delirium; it induced mental inertia, so that you became almost comatose. Anyway, it was designed to make God as boring as possible. Bore. It bored into your brain as you recited the names of these long-forgotten saints and people of the past: the wonderful double act of the Roman amphitheatre, 'Cosmos and Damien'; the now relegated St Philomena, and a host of others who are long since lost to memory. Ah, happy days; well, actually, incredibly boring days.

But I am now a convert to litanies. I have made my own list of new and startling saints. They include, first and foremost, my incredibly generous family and friends who have supported us in this little enterprise; without them, the experience could not have happened. There are all the people of the VMM in Liverpool, Dublin, Kiltegan, who were, are, unforgettable. Some of them have now gone on to other things, but the inspiration they gave! The gang of '78, who are scattered all over the globe, are forever burned into my brain. The excitement of knowing and growing with them was sheer joy. The people who we met over here: other volunteers from other organisations, the youngsters, the oldsters; what a privilege to be with them and to know them. To use a phrase my young American friends use over here, 'awesome'. They were indeed awesome. Then the staff of the school, especially Betty the head, and the superb and wonderful evergreen Sisters of Laverna. But most of all the girls of St Clare.

The girls. My girls. Extraordinary. This is my list of saints; this is my litany. Not dead, or unknown, or obscure, but vibrant, alive, a company of living, breathing life. Wonderful saints. I recite their names with joy.

Printed in the United Kingdom
by Lightning Source UK Ltd.
123750UK00001B/81/A